EXPLORING YOUR UNCONSCIOUS MIND

And it shall come to pass afterward,
That I will pour out my spirit upon all
flesh; and your sons and your daughters
shall prophesy, your old men shall dream
dreams, your young men shall see visions.

Joel 2:28

EXPLORING YOUR UNCONSCIOUS MIND

FORMERLY ENTITLED A TRIP INTO YOUR UNCONSCIOUS

W.A. MAMBERT
B. FRANK FOSTER

CORNERSTONE LIBRARY   NEW YORK

Reprinted 1977

*This new Cornerstone Library edition is published by arrangement
with ACROPOLIS BOOKS LTD. and is a complete and unabridged
reprint of the original hardcover edition formerly entitled A Trip Into
Your Unconscious.*

ISBN: 346-12322-4

Manufactured in the United States of America
under the supervision of
Rolls Offset Printing Co. Inc. N. Y.

Contents

Foreword

As I read *A Trip Into Your Unconscious*, the book attracted me because here the "trip" was not dependent upon drugs or upon potentially disturbing or disastrous encounter group experiences. Those seeking a "trip" for "mind-expanding," inner self-understanding, and a knowledge of the deeper and unconscious influences upon their behavior will find a wealth of information. And those wanting a "trip" for self-improvement will find many guidelines.

This book is written for the layman. In the definitions of professional psychology and psychiatry it is also written by laymen. For some time I have known W. A. Mambert as an applied psychologist. He has contributed to the field of business and human living a superb knowledge of the psychology of human communication. The other author, B. Frank Foster, who was killed in an airplane accident before the completion of the book, I did not know. He contributes the religious approaches and emphases. The book merges the two authors' philosophies very well. The discussions of the inner mind and dreams are interwoven with the philosophies of life and experiences of these two applied psychologists—one of the business world and one of the church.

To many the book will represent their first meeting with Jungian psychoanalytical concepts and theories related to the unconscious and to dreams. The broader outcome of reading this book might well be a desire to pursue further these concepts and theories, as well as to delve into other psychoanalytic and psychological approaches to understanding the unconscious and dreams.

Current psychological thinking emphasizes self-understanding, self-analyzing, rationalizing, self-actualizing approaches. This book addresses itself to such interests. Its basic appeal will lie in the intrinsically appealing nature of its subject matter—the inner mind and dreams. It can be recommended for dealing with a neglected source of self-understanding—dreams.

A Trip Into Your Unconscious will attract readers who are seeking to understand themselves in a variety of ways. It can be recommended for its fresh emphases upon old approaches and can be commended for its eclectic secular and religious approach.

As a professional psychologist and psychiatrist writing this Foreword, I must caution against self-analyzing as a substitute for professional assistance where needed. But to end with a positive note where it may seem I introduced a negative one—adequate self-understanding is the best guarantee of good psychological adjustment and mental health. This book should be a positive influence.

Thelma Hunt, Ph.D., M.D.

The George Washington University

1

The Most Profitable Learning

You would be a rare person indeed if you did not sense the stresses and frustrations of our times. For all of us are swept up in an era that has produced a more desperate and urgent need for personal redemption and regenerative experience than at any other time in history. The psychiatrist's couch sees only the tip of the iceberg—the relatively few persons who can no longer bear alone their inner turmoil, and who turn to their fellow man for help. The rest of us merely go from day to day, some of us managing a little better than others. But all of us are secretly yearning to live more fully with an inner peace, dignity, independence, and nobleness of spirit that something within us senses ought to be.

What, after all, are the real questions that confront each of us? Isn't the single most urgent issue of life the question of how much inner harmony we can obtain as we live our lives? It is somewhat paradoxical that the "secret" of obtaining this inner peace and rectitude has been around almost as long as man has been looking for it. Read the ancient Egyptians, the Hebrews, the Persians, the Chinese, the Greeks and Romans, the thinkers and the writers of the Renaissance and the Enlightenment, or the tenets of modern psychiatry. Always, you will hear the same refrain. Yet the vast majority of us seem deaf and blind to what has been known for centuries to be the only safe and certain first step to personal victory in life.

What is this great secret? There is no point in overcomplicating the matter. Strip away all of the psychological mumbo-jumbo, all of the fancy and high sounding theological interpretation and exposition, all of the philosophical esotericism, and you are left with the simple but profound precept coined so long ago: "know thyself." Self-knowledge is the beginning of all other meaningful knowing. It is, as the fifteenth century ecclesiastic Thomas a Kempis echoed the ancient refrain, "the highest and most profitable learning." It is the beginning of all self-help, all personal growth, all psychic therapy, all self-adjustment, and all personal regeneration.

" 'Know thyself,' " wrote the ancient Roman philospher Cicero, "was not solely intended to obviate the pride of mankind; but likewise that we might understand our own worth," our own place in the scheme of things. "The superior man," said the venerable Chinese philosopher Confucius, "will watch over himself when he is alone. He examines his heart that there be nothing wrong there, and that he may have no cause for dissatisfaction with himself." The Biblical proverbist said, "As a man thinketh in his heart, so is he." The New Testament writers admonished that if any man would know God, he must first "confess his sins," that is, admit to and know his own self. The seventeenth century philosopher Alexander Pope wrote, "Any man who sets out to cure the ills of the world by not first altering his *own disposition of mind* will only multiply the ills that he sets out to cure." C.G. Jung, for modern man, states, "only when the individual is willing to fulfill the demands of rigorous self-examination and self-knowledge" can there be any meaningful connection with the rest of the real world, or even with God, however anyone defines "Him."

The problem for most of us does not lie in accepting the basic precept that self-knowledge is our key to the "pursuit of happiness." Our problem is that many of us do not know how to go beyond more than a superficial level to get this self-knowledge.

A doctor once mentioned to the authors how consistently amazed he is at how little people know about the "bodies in which they live." The average person, for example, knows far more about the ignition system of his automobile than he knows about his own heart, or his liver, or his lungs. The same sort of thing might be said about the average person and his own mind and thinking processes. Most of us are not familiar with the "psychic territory" in which we live. Yet, we yearn to know the mysteries of our own selves. As Gibran's *Prophet* put it, we long to touch with our fingers the naked body of our dreams.

For example, the average person tends to think of self-knowledge as what he consciously perceives and knows. But in truth, your "self" is, as the same poet put it, a "sea, boundless and deep." There is at least as much of you, and probably more, "beneath the surface," hidden from your conscious observation, as there is above. It is when you have the tools to explore these hidden reaches of your own mind that you begin to *truly* discover your whole self and your potential.

Any serious attempt at self-knowledge must, therefore, begin with at least some knowledge of the nature and extent of the whole self. That is, we must have some understanding of our own psychic composition. When the average layman hears the term "psychic," he may think primarily in terms of the fictional, the mystical or the occult, perhaps of the world of mediums, fortunetellers, clairvoyants, and "twilight zones." While it is true that "psychic" does include this mystical connotation as a part of, shall we say, its upper or outer ranges, the *psyche* is a very practical and highly inclusive concept to the working psychologist, psychiatrist or psychoanalyst—all of whom, incidentally, derive the names of their professions from the term itself. It should be the same to any person who wishes to analyze and thus know himself better.

Literally, *psyche* means "soul" or "life-force," or the "principle of life." Some psychologists today use the term as an equivalent of "mind." Some use it as a substitute for the "unconscious" or "subconscious." All such connotations seem too restrictive. A more enlightened approach would be to see the term in a more encompassing and inclusive sense than any of these, more in the sense of its original Greek meaning, but also in an open-ended way. We must not close our minds to what our psychic makeup might yet be discovered to include. We should be open-minded and see the psychic realm as a kind of spectrum or range encompassing the total self. It includes the deep, primitive, instinctive urges and drives within the self. It also may include the rational, thinking, socialized being and processes, and even the so-called spiritual experiencing of life.

Your *psyche*, then, is the sum of many things. It is, as the Greeks originally put it, the life force in you. It is the soul of you, the tangible and conscious you and the unconscious and intangible you. And this is how we use the term here: to signify the composite of your conscious and unconscious being and personality—your instincts, intuition, sensations, feelings, emotions, urges, memories and experiences, as well as your connection to all other human beings who have preceded you, and to a larger, perhaps divine, force, or "law of nature." Your *psyche* is a whole that is greater than the sum of its parts. It includes both the known and observable and the unknown and unobservable—that which can only be experienced, but not quantified. *Psyche* is far less "yours" than it is *you*. The possessive is used here merely as a communicative device.

C. G. Jung was one of the early psychoanalysts who dealt with the nature of the psyche. We find much of his terminology useful in trying to identify the concepts you should understand as a basis for self-analysis. The most important of these are the following:

The Conscious	The Shadow
The Unconscious	The Persona
The Collective Unconscious	Repression and Complex Formation
The Animus and Anima	The Superconscious

THE IMPORTANCE OF WHOLENESS

It is extremely important never to think of these concepts as separate and discrete "partitions" or "compartments" in the human mind or psyche. We not only speak of the undiscovered self, we must speak of the unseparated self. Probably the greatest single mistake made throughout the history of man's struggle to understand himself, since the recording of the very myth of the Creation in the Book of Genesis, has been the *separation of self*, the fragmentation of the unity of man. Interestingly, sensitive thinkers have also known this for centuries. Here is a passage by William Blake, the eighteenth century philosopher.*

> All Bibles or sacred codes have been the cause of the following errors—
> 1. That man has two real existing principles, viz., a body and a soul.

*From *The Marriage of Heaven and Hell*.

2. That energy, called evil, is alone from the body; and that reason, called good, is alone from the soul.
3. That God will torment man in eternity for following his energies

But the following contraries to these are true—

1. Man has no body distinct from his soul. For that called body is a portion of soul discerned by the five senses, the chief inlets of the soul in this age.
2. Energy is the only life, and is from the body; and reason is the bound or outward circumference of energy.

It is most interesting to the student of history to see that in almost every age of man, wherever thoughtful, truth-seeking men have sought to understand the nature of man, they have run upon the same fundamental truths. The above is a case in point.

For, as one's understanding of one's own conscious and unconscious self develops, one sees that there is very little difference between this thought expressed nearly two hundred years ago and the modern psychiatric theory of *complex development*. Understanding your own complexes is a major part of fully understanding your whole self. As the "complex," or the deviation from what we commonly call normal behavior, is understood today, it is precisely what Blake saw as man's "following of his energies." That is, much so-called abnormal behavior is not unnatural or abnormal behavior at all, but merely an overactivity of a perfectly normal and natural energy within a person's makeup. For example, it is quite normal for a human being to be ego-defensive. His ego-defensive behavior becomes a complex, or is considered abnormal, when it becomes, for some reason, overactive, when it intensifies into perhaps paranoia or undue suspicion of other people.

Blake and other earlier thinkers saw the dangers in arbitrarily separating the nature of man into "parts," of negating his wholeness, of making people feel needlessly guilty for doing nothing more than being natural human beings. We think of the number of men and women who have grown up in a Puritanistic environment in the last two or three centuries, who have lived lives of misery and despair, of guilt and frustration, of unfulfillment, simply because misguided religionists taught them from childhood that being human was a "sin," and that half or more of their *natural* impulses were not a justifiable part of their selves and would condemn them to hell fire. So it has gone, and so it goes to this day. Drs. Franz G. Alexander and Sheldon T. Selesnick, authors of *The History of Psychiatry*, appropriately reaffirm that the greatest mistake in the thinking of Western Man has undoubtedly been his theoretical separation of his own nature into body and soul, good and evil, natural and unnatural, etc. Most modern psychologists now echo the same message. Unity-wholeness-harmony are evident throughout the whole of the universe. Why should man be an exception? Therefore, as you read on, do not think of each element of the human self as something separate and apart from all of the others, but all as parts of each other and of the whole person, remembering that the quest for wholeness is in fact the ultimate aim of the whole study of man. If, in fact, you remember nothing else from reading this chapter, remember that you owe no man, nor God, an apology for being a human being.

THE INDIVIDUATED PERSON

If you ask a young person today what he has been doing lately, he is likely to say, "I've been trying to get it together." What he is really saying is that he has been trying to get *himself* together." He has been seeking that wholeness of which we just spoke. The Jungian term *individuation* is a good one to describe the process by which a person becomes a psychologically integrated whole—a unique and homogeneous entity capable of solving his problems, coping successfully with his environment—and of that full "pursuit of happiness." In the final analysis, too, it is only this personal fulfillment that can lead to any meaningful and lastingly workable collective human ideal.

CONFRONTING SELF

For most people this process of individuation, of becoming mature and whole, involves as its very first step one of the most distasteful chores that can be assigned to a human being—the task of self-confrontation. An act of will and volition is involved. Before proceeding, one must take a realistic look at himself as he is. Any person who wants to take any further steps toward *any* personal growth must take this step first. Make no mistake, it is not an easy step. But it *must* be taken. If, in fact, you are not willing or ready to take it, you needn't read further in this book.

As already pointed out, we do not speak here of a mere surface confrontation, obtaining only a frontal view in a mirror. We speak of looking in and past that one-dimensional image into your complete inner self. We speak of looking into the whole world of self, where there is no excuse for what exists or is seen, and where *no excuse is needed.* And you must particularly remember this. Probably one of the main reasons that most people do not look more deeply into themselves is that they do indeed feel guilty for what they might find. This simply is not necessary. It says in the Bible that "God looks at the inner man." If God already sees the inner man, what could you possibly see that could surprise Him before whom you presumably "ought" to feel guilty? And if you do not believe in God, before whom else do you stand guilty? Other people? Posh! They are as "guilty" as you—guilty of being humans—no more, no less. It has often been our urge in personal counseling to come right out and say to a person struggling against his own needless guilt, "Come now. Stop this foolishness! So you're human, and you have many selves within you. So what! Let's get down to the business of seeing what they need and want in order to become useful and helpful to the rest of you." Sometimes we do say this. But often we don't because we know that it is such a painful process for many people, *needless* as that pain may be. People are not always ready to hear this. So, we try to be gentle, to open eyes gradually, to let a little light in at a time. As the Bible says, "with fear and trembling" men "work out their salvation."

THE MOMENT OF SHOCK

In the actual process of *individuation*—the coming to terms of your conscious and inner selves—when you first confront yourself and realize what you really are, there usually is a distinct and identifiable moment of psychic shock. As Jung puts it, there is a "wounding of the personality." We would not have you believe that there is not usually some suffering involved in self-knowledge. This is true not only at the first moment of self-confrontation, but throughout the ensuing process of self-examination. This shock phenomenon is well known to psychotherapists. Close on its heels comes a second phenomenon, known as *projection*. As you look into yourself, unless you are already an individuated person, your first response will actually be to find "nothing that needs fixing."

In fact, you probably will find that it is the external system, the economy, some other person, or even God who is at fault. *You* will project your own shortcomings upon someone else. The key is to go beyond, penetrate this "shock wave," *enter* into the world of your unconscious and deeper self where you can see things as they really are. And this is merely where the adventure of individuation begins. The more discoveries about yourself that you make, the freer you become from your own hang-ups and the things that prevent you from being a truly free and responsible individual. Be prepared for this initial shock, recognize it when it occurs. The surest sign that you are up against it will be when you are most clearly able to see the faults of others as you look into yourself.

THE NEED FOR OBJECTIVITY

No book about self-analysis would be complete without some mention of the necessity for personal objectivity. Niccolo Machiavelli, the sixteenth century Italian political philosopher, is often looked at in a negative way for the autocratic political views he expressed in *The Prince*. But he said at least one thing that makes good sense for any person trying to analyze or deal with a problem or body of information. "I prefer," he said, "to deal with things as they really are, and not as we might wish them to be."

Without a capability to resolve to step occasionally outside of yourself, and to observe yourself as another person might see you, you will have extreme difficulty in obtaining any view of what is happening inside you that will be truly useful in altering those happenings.

Accept, then, the validity of your own wholeness as a psychic entity and the possibility that there may be parts of you that are now separated from that wholeness. Realize, too, that when we speak of self-knowledge in this book, we are talking about more than what a person perceives at the conscious level. We speak, rather, of a knowledge of the whole self.

We should also clearly point out here that we do not speak of self-knowledge in terms of the norms of mass man. Individuated persons are, and to some extent ought to be, governed in their sense of self by an awareness of how they fit among other people. But, we speak of the self-knowledge that does not use *any* criterion for the way things within one's self "ought" to be. We speak of your discovery of *the way it is within you*, no matter how it is or ought to be outside of you. This is the self-knowledge that is "the highest and most profitable learning."

When I was a child, my speech, my outlook, and my thoughts were all childish. When I grew up, I had finished with childish things. Now we see only puzzling reflections in a mirror, but then we shall see face to face. My knowledge now is partial; then it will be whole, like God's knowledge of me.
1 Corinthians 13:10-13

2
Understanding Your Conscious Self

In realistic self-analysis, the best place to begin is with an understanding of your conscious mind. There are at least four good reasons for this. First, your conscious mind represents the most familiar territory. Second, its contents are the most available information. Third, much of the information in your conscious mind is of a literal, instead of figurative or symbolic, nature and can be understood without translation or interpretation. As we shall see later, this is not always true of the inner, unconscious parts of your mind which often "speak" in a symbolic or allegorical way requiring interpretation. Fourth, an objective understanding of your conscious behavior often will give you important clues to how your inner self is behaving and what it is "saying" to you.

Like the term psyche, "conscious" may mean one thing to the layman and another to the scientific observer of human personality and behavior. Also like *psyche*, psychoanalytically speaking, *conscious* is a very inclusive and encompassing descriptive term. It is more than just being

Thinking is the primary function of the conscious and the

awake or not having "lost consciousness" in the medical or physiological sense. We will begin by saying that it is fundamentally the state of wakefulness and awareness, and much more. Your conscious is the *total waking you*. It should come as no surprise that not only are a great many people unacquainted with their inner selves, many are not very well acquainted with their outer, or conscious, selves either. They may know what they consciously *think*, but they give very little thought to *why* they think or to the actual mechanisms of their consciousness. We must, however, understand the structure and aspects of our outer, conscious self before becoming able to understand the workings of our inner, unconscious self and its activities. In fact, the simultaneous understanding of both the unconscious and the conscious is better yet. As we have said, there is no clear line of demarcation. Talk of "separate parts" of the human psyche gives the wrong impression. Because what you are really looking at, when you observe the conscious and unconscious you, is something more like a blended mixture which graphically illustrated might look something like a marble cake or several streams of varicolored oil or water flowing together. The conscious exists simultaneously and continuously with the unconscious. The two are continually intermingling, interacting and "flowing together." The manifestations of this interacting coexistence are quite readily observable.

THE FUNCTIONS OF CONCIOUSNESS

Borrowing from Jung's analysis of mental activity, consciousness can be thought of as manifesting itself in four basic functions: *thinking, feeling, intuition*, and *sensation*. Following are descriptions of what we mean by these terms:

Thinking

Thinking is the primary function of the conscious and the

one with which most of us feel familiar. It is the voluntary and largely intentional use of the mind to adapt to the circumstances and stimuli that confront it in waking life. It is our coping and dealing with life through the rationalizing process and the use of what we commonly call intelligence. Many of us, mainly because we normally don't stop to think about what is going on in our minds, merely "do the thing," and tend to regard this as the sum and substance of our consciousness. Actually, this thinking function is a relatively small part of our consciousness. In a larger sense, it is not even confined to the thinking process per se; that is, merely the "thinking out" in terms of observation, logic and conscious problem solving. For the thinking function also operates in the sense of *reacting* at the mental level, whether or not any logic or thinking is involved. It includes, for example, all of the behavior patterns we have developed to deal with specific, repetitive situations in life, the kind of things one does without stopping to think.

It is in this latter realm, also, that the interaction of the conscious and the unconscious becomes almost immediately apparent. For example, you consciously drive a car, but in actuality your unconscious is partially driving the car too. As you think, work, study, interact with other people, etc., at what we normally think of as the conscious level, the conscious mind is continually "pulling up" pre-established rational thought and behavior patterns that were not immediately apparent to it only a moment before. The simple act of remembering is, in fact, an interaction of the conscious and unconscious.

Feeling

Feeling is another level, or function, of the conscious. There is a range of reaction and behavior at the conscious level that does not come under the heading of thinking as we normally use the term, and yet which also is based upon a rational system of making value judgments. We speak here basically of that part of our mental behavior in which both the rationale and the emotions intermix to cause us to react, have opinions, and experience "feelings." Thinking, as described above, is based upon a true-false rationale; while feeling is based upon a pleasurable-unpleasurable rationale. Both, therefore, are in the rational realm. For example, we like or dislike certain things, fear something, feel an affinity toward a person, or have a value judgment toward something. We do not speak here, either of that which is intuitive, for example, having a hunch or premonition. This is not deliberate and not based on any kind of rationale. This feeling process is essentially a reasoning one and therefore more logically described as a part of the rational as opposed to the nonrational processes of the mind.

Intuition

Intuition is a traditional term which Jung adopted to mean a specific thing in speaking of the conscious as opposed to the unconscious. It has to do with involuntary, nonrationalized responses as opposed to the thought-out response. It corresponds rather closely to the modern terminology of "getting the vibrations" in a given situation or set of circumstances. Intuition, as Jung used the term, describes those responses and feelings that arise into the conscious mind unbidden, such as the premonition or the hunch. It depends upon an entirely different set of stimuli, processes and conditions than either thinking or feeling. Whereas thinking and feeling represent a voluntary putting together of things consciously seen, experienced, or remembered, intuition is totally involuntary. It would be hard for us to control our intuition if we wanted to. Of all of the functions of the conscious, this range is most closely connected and related to the unconscious. Its workings may or may not be stimulated by something in the conscious.

The average person, busy as his conscious mind is with the here-and-now mechanisms of living and responding to the conditions around him, is likely to pass over or ignore much of his own intuitive activity. Usually, at best, the spontaneous arising into his conscious mind of some aspect of his intuitiveness manifests itself in perhaps a vague feeling of uneasiness, nostalgia, perhaps the "blues," or simply a hunch. These days, hunches and premonitions don't count for much. After all, we are rational beings (we keep telling ourselves). We deal with the "facts." If, however, we understood a little more of the real nature and genesis of this intuitiveness, we might be a little less disposed to ignore it. This can be appreciated more when one comes to understand the structure and functions of both the unconscious and the conscious. For, in actuality, your intuitiveness springs from much deeper than the purely conscious level. Your hunches, moods, your sudden "flashes" or your mental images, may in reality be "messages" emerging from your broader base of experience and reasoning powers. The key is to get back in touch with and to trust this part of the greater, whole you.

One of the best statements of the value of tapping this inner "well of discipline" can be found in the book, *On Becoming A Person*, by the noted psychologist, Carl R. Rogers. The authors tend to place some weight on the words of men like Rogers, who has practiced psychology for thirty-five years and has helped thousands of people. To begin his book, Rogers lists what he says have been his "significant learnings" over his lifetime of intimate association with individual human ills, hopes, desires, fears, and other dysfunctions. One of his most significant learnings, he says, has been that he has come to trust his own "feelings." If he feels a thing is of value and worth doing, regardless of what the intellectual processes might say, it usually proves to be worth doing. What he really has said is that he has learned to trust his *intuition*, his vibrations, the total experience of himself as a person. Most mature persons sooner or later come to this realization, to an awareness that some combination of the voice within and the intellect is warranted. As William James put it, the *full* meaning of things is more likely the result of the full inner, intuitive range of response than of any ratiocination.

Sensation

The physical-receiving mechanisms of the body also are a part of the conscious. Almost all human experiences originally enter into and become a part of the total psychic makeup through one or some combination of the five senses. It might help to think of your self as a kind of storehouse of impressions, feelings, and experiences. Your senses are the input mechanisms which gather these things. Both your conscious and your unconscious store them away. You may think that you "forget" them. But what probably happens is that your conscious turns them over to your unconscious. So far as psychologists can determine, there is much evidence that somewhere within you there is a "record" of everything you have heard, seen, tasted, smelled and felt. Knowledge of this will become increasingly significant to you as you read on.

Jung used an interesting and easily understood explanation and graphic representation of the individuation process that should help us here also. The four functions just described—thinking, feeling, intuition and sensation—represent all the known possibilities of conscious activity. There are, of course, many other ways of classifying and typing what these terms represent. The ancient Greeks, for example, classified human beings by various "humours" or fluids that flowed within the body; namely, blood (sanguine); black bile (melancholic); bile (choleric); and phlegm (phlegmatic). One frequently still encounters this terminology in conversation and literature today. The Greeks spoke in terms of the body fluids flowing in harmony, in balance. They claimed their typology to be complete. Jung, however, merely stated that his typology is the best available according to what is presently known—a basic difference between the earlier and the modern thinker. Whatever they are called, Jung confirmed that if the various conscious functions could be brought into a balanced and harmonious continuing interaction with each other, a greater personal adjustment would ensue.

Put another way, human maladjustment and dysfunctioning occur when one of the functions of the conscious unduly dominates. One philosopher put it quite aptly in saying that many of man's troubles stem from the fact that he usually is thinking when he should be feeling, and feeling when he should be thinking. In the individual human being, it is likely that, through environmental influence, one function may overdevelop at the expense of the others, thus developing an abnormal personality type, or, a person partially out of touch with parts of himself. The result is that one winds up as a "personality type." For example, there is the type of person who operates almost entirely "from the neck up." He rationalizes everything that happens to him. He cannot feel. He is unaware of his own feelings, let alone those of others. He can be cruel and insensitive. On the other hand, a person whose feeling function is overdeveloped may respond irrationally. The "sensation" personality, in turn, may function too much at the physical level, neglecting both his thinking and feeling responses. And the intuitive type is likely to turn out as a completely unreliable "scatterbrain." Interestingly, this type of distortion often seems to occur not only at the individual level, but at the level of whole cultures and societies as well; for example, at times when certain "social moods" or "temperaments" such as mass fear, apathy, irrationality, etc., grip large segments of a society.

Most readers today have no doubt been exposed to the ideas of "sensitivity," "awareness," "T," and similar groups, and the movement they represent. The popular idea of the intensified group experience is, among other things, an example of how a social movement or trend can spontaneously grow out of a deep, collective social need. The conscious functions are not *merely* functions, but represent human needs and drives as well. They have roots that go much deeper than the conscious level of our beings. When such needs and drives are not fulfilled, they always seem to "try" in one way or another to assert themselves or make themselves known, thus lending credibility to the idea that deep inside every human being there exist many urges common to all, such as a primitive, instinctual urge to be whole. When a social phenomenon such as technology or scientific rationalism occurs through the interaction of other collective human forces stronger than any single individual, it can work to thwart these basic needs and urges at the collective, as well as the individual human level. The result is what Jacques Barzun, the noted American educator, called a "lopsided" society.

This is basically what has happened to us today. We live in a society that operates essentially from the neck up. The emphasis is cearly upon the thinking function (Figure 2-1). Yet, deep within every person remains the need to fulfill the other functions—feeling, sensing, and intuitiveness. It is partially out of this collective need that the intensified group experience movement has emerged. Vast numbers of people today, driven (although they may not have analyzed the reasons for it) by their deep need to be whole again, flock to such groups because this is a need they fulfill.

The outsider may wonder why these groups seem to concentrate on "touching," letting people express any feeling that comes to them, telling of their dreams, reacting spontaneously, etc. These things are not *over*emphasized in

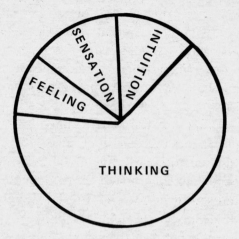

Figure 2-1. Technological man has overdeveloped his thinking, or rational, function at the expense of his capabilities for feeling, intuition and sensation. Rationalization takes up more than its share of the whole person. As individual man goes, so goes society.

these groups. They have been *under*emphasized by the rest of society. The group experience merely seeks to retrain what may have become vestigial in modern man—the ability to feel, to be fully aware of what his senses are telling him, to listen to his inner voices, as well as to think and rationalize.

The intensified group experience, therefore, may be viewed as modern man's answer to getting the "humours" back into a balanced flow. The mass media, as they usually do, have given a partially false picture of what such groups are really about. They emphasize the groups' bizarre and unconventional aspects. And, of course, there are a few charlatans involved, as usually is the case with any good thing. The authors recommend that the reader himself obtain firsthand evidence, based on a knowledge of the underlying theory, before reaching any conclusion.

In any case, the basic aim of the intensified group experience is to help individual people to become whole again, to relearn the process of *fully* experiencing what life has to offer the "sensitive" and "aware" person who makes full use of *all* his conscious and unconscious capabilities.

According to Jung, we might look at the whole personality of an adjusted person as a circular disc with the main conscious functions arranged in quadrants as shown in Figure 2-2. The difference between the adjusted and unadjusted person is that the conscious functions are more-equally present and operating. You can go even a step further in this illustration. Assume that each quadrant is a different color. If you were to cut this disc out, place a pin in its center, and spin it so that the colors merged and blended, you would have some idea of Jung's concept of individuation, a proper mix of all the conscious functions (Figure 2-3).

THE FOUR FUNCTIONS AND THE UNCONSCIOUS

As just explained, these functions are not only functions, they also are deep *needs* within the personality. Like other inherent human needs, if you do not adequately fulfill them, they will continually try to assert themselves in both your unconscious and conscious behavior. They can appear in dreams, for example, in the form of *shadow figures* (explained later), or in dream *activities* that a person is too inhibited to engage in while awake. They also can appear in what seems to be inconsistent or "irrational" waking behavior; even in body language—the way we walk, stand, sit, hold our bodies, etc.

A STATE OF CONTINUOUS CHANGE

Your conscious is not a passive, inert, quantifiable entity either. It is rather a continuously changing and expanding fact. It grows and expands with experience from infancy to adulthood. One may get the impression from the preceding descriptions that the conscious is to be regarded as merely a division of labor within the mind. But this is only a part of

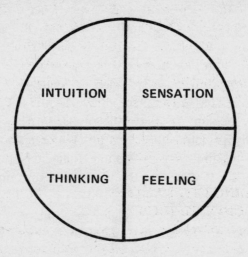

Figure 2-2. A graphic representation of the four conscious functions in equal proportion.

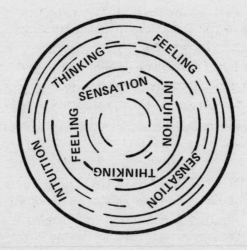

Figure 2-3. The *individuated* person "spins" his personality, merging all of his conscious functions in a healthy, balanced way.

the picture. The conscious represents both a *process* of information and experience gathering and a part of the *knowledge* or memory of that information and experience. As the sum of what is wakefully known or experienced (mentally, emotionally, sensorially and intuitively at any given moment), it might be better described as a *process of interrelating* with the world. In other words, your conscious is the total waking you and your identity, at least the identity of which you are aware.

A CONTINUING INTERACTION WITH THE UNCONSCIOUS

Your conscious and unconscious are continually interacting with each other when you are both awake and asleep. Dreams, for example, are an interaction between the unconscious and the conscious. Your conscious not only feeds information to your unconscious. The reverse also is true. Your unconscious is continually feeding information to your conscious. This is basically what happens in dreaming. A part of the individuation process is when a person becomes more *aware* of the information that is flowing or has flowed in both directions, when a dialogue between the conscious and unconscious is established. This is of primary importance in psychotherapy. Because so long as information remains in the unconscious, no one—therapist or patient—knows what it is, and it cannot be dealt with. One of the main aims in therapy is to make conscious that which was unconscious, the long forgotten memory, the stored or repressed impression or experience. Once at the conscious level these can be dealt with. This is why dream interpretation is such a great help in psychotherapy. For the dream does make known to the conscious what was formerly known only to the unconscious.

In the next chapter, we shall see more of how your conscious is influenced and often involuntarily controlled by your unconscious. For the moment, however, let us look a little further in the other direction—at how your conscious communicates with and uses information stored in your unconscious.

There are several types of interrelated mental activities which occur primarily in the normal waking state that represent interactions of the conscious and unconscious. In our present action- and fact-oriented society, some of these activities have acquired a negative connotation. When you understand what is really happening, however, you will find that such activities represent natural and often valuable functions of your mind.

Daydreaming

To "daydream" or to "fantasize," for example, is generally considered to be a useless pastime. The employee or student caught gazing out of the window usually is made to feel guilty, even held up to ridicule, because he has permitted his mind to wander from the here and now. Like night dreams, however, daydreams can provide important information to the person who is willing to observe their contents and treat them as valid data, which they are. Some clinical research has been done on daydreams at the City University of New York and at the University of Illinois. Researchers have found, among other things, some correlations of certain types of daydreams with neuroses, autistic behavior and other personality dysfunctions.

There also are some positive benefits of daydreaming in so-called normal people. Studies of human creativity, in particular, have revealed that creative types are more disposed to this activity, and that it definitely seems to help them by heightening their awareness and developing their creativity. Other studies have shown that intentionally induced daydreaming has a positive tranquilizing or relaxing effect on personal anxiety.

Daydreaming, like several of the other activities listed here, can therefore be viewed as a resource of the human mind. Its analysis can produce a needed awareness of personal faults or failures. It also is just plain relaxing and entertaining. At the very least, daydreaming should be considered as a source of information about what is happening in the human mind.

Fantasy

As with daydreaming, some serious research has also been conducted on the tendency in humans to produce mental fantasies. Researchers at the University of Washington found some interesting results. For example, they discovered that fantasizing seemed to reduce inner anger and hostility in people by working these things out in a harmless way. Most of us have had fantasizing experiences. One of the most common is associated with movies or other works of fiction. Hero worship and identification with or imitation of particularly desirable fictional characters is not uncommon. For most of us, this identification or imitation fades within a few blocks from the movie theater, or shortly after the book is put down. Yet, the experience is not without potential benefit. For analysis of the characteristics with which we identify can give some information as to actual "gaps" in our own development. It is rare, for example, for people who have already reached a certain status or level of development to fantasize and identify with fictional characters who are portrayed as having reached similar stages.

Thus, what you frequently may have in the fantasy, and often in the daydream, is an object example of some of your own shortcomings—a "message" about psychic areas in which you may need some adjustment. Fantasy and daydreaming obviously are quite similar and often overlap in definition and content. If there is a main difference, it is that daydreaming seems to start more spontaneously than fantasizing, which more often starts as the result of some external stimulus. In either case, they both seem to have a definite function in the personality, and both provide data that should at least be considered in any realistic self-analysis.

Visions

We speak here of the type of hallucinatory occurrence usually associated with religious experience. There are many records of these in the Bible and throughout history, particularly in the Catholic faith, usually associated with the Virgin Mary. It is of interest that so-called visions usually occur in people who are "ready" for them. For example, the recorded visions of the Virgin have occurred almost exclusively with Catholics. Certain times in history seem to produce more visions than others do, usually when there is a widespread fear or deep-seated "temper of the times."

One things is certain: visions do occur. And, as often as not, they occur in the lives of the most reputable of people. Aside from Jung, few researchers have treated them as anything more than another form of hallucination. Jung, however, examined the visions of numerous well-educated and intelligent people, treating them as a scientist would treat any other observable phenomenon. He saw them as highly symbolic representations of some very deep fears and cravings occurring in individuals. We will not come right out and say here that visions are "messages from God" or from the "God force" within man. Yet, visions at an individual level often emerge from—and portray—not only personal hopes and fears, but the terrors, fears or hopes of a larger segment of society within a given era. And, of course, the average individual has a relatively narrow comprehension of the "God idea" or the "God force," and is likely to think solely in anthropomorphic terms when speaking of messages from God. We prefer the view that the "voice" of God may take many forms and refrain from reinventing Him in our own image.

Meditation

The practice of meditation, a common human activity for many centuries, also exhibits many characteristics that relate it to the unconscious. Meditation is different from any of the waking activities described thus far in that it is an *intentionally* self-induced state and method of "dipping into" what is stored in the more-hidden recesses of the mind. Striking is the great overall similarity of the methods of meditation across the lines of many cultures and many times. The mechanics of meditation have changed little from the earliest recorded days. Most forms of meditation are based upon a repetitious process designed to shut out as many external sensory stimuli as possible. This restricts input to the brain and permits its powers to be concentrated. Brain wave readings of people meditating are very similar to those of people in the dreaming state. Usually the person meditating begins by focusing and concentrating all of his senses on a single item, such as a candle flame, a mandala, a sacred object, a real or imaginary spot. This keeping of a single object in consciousness, at the exclusion of as many others as possible, produces a certain state, which is meditation, in which the contents of the unconscious mind have a greater opportunity to become known.

People who have mastered the art of meditation sometimes are actually able to "turn off" their vision and hearing, even to slow down their pulses and heartbeats, much as in the sleeping state. There is a definite relaxing of anxiety in such a state. There is a pronounced increase in inner perceptions. The contents of deeper parts of the mind are often seen with an increased clarity and understanding, and there is a resultant general pacification of the whole human mechanism.

Remembering

Most people probably don't think of the simple act of remembering at the conscious level as associated with the unconscious mind. A moment's reflection, however, may modify this view. When you remember something that you have not been thinking of a moment before, where does it come from? It was not in your conscious mind. Therefore it must have been somewhere else, but still within you. What has really happened is that your conscious mind has "accessed" the deeper storehouse of information beneath your immediate awareness; in other words, your unconscious. As we shall see in more detail in the following chapters, the unconscious has a much more significant role in conscious activity than we might realize. It exists at different levels and strata within us, with some of its contents easily accessible and others hidden and less accessible to the conscious.

Habits and Automatic Behavior

The professional psychiatrist has very sophisticated meanings for such terms as "habit" and "habituation." We do not need to worry about these definitions here. We are merely talking about the fact that conscious activity includes an interlayering and interaction of both forgotten experiences and those things of which we are aware at any given moment. Processes that the conscious repeats over and over again disappear from our immediate awareness. When we are first learning the little complexities of a conscious activity, we are fully aware of them. As we repeat them, become conditioned to doing them, they become automatic. The conscious takes on what amounts to a monitoring role. Certain sensory stimuli call forth a whole pattern of action or reaction, of which we are not fully aware. This also illustrates how the senses relate to the unconscious as well as the conscious. The simple act of walking down the street is an example. It uses parts of both the conscious and unconscious mind. Using the conscious sensing mechanisms, we can stop at a crossing, guide around people and obstacles, even reach our destinations without complete conscious awareness of what we are doing. We can walk into a room with a ticking clock and take no note of its sound, yet "know" that it is ticking. When it stops ticking, we suddenly become aware that at some level of our consciousness, and perhaps our unconscious as well, we had been perceiving and recording the occurrence all along.

Much of such habituation serves a useful function. It enables our conscious minds to operate on more than one "channel" at a time and thus to get better use of our time. Other habituation may reveal less desirable patterns of thinking and behavior. People in awareness and sensitivity groups frequently help each other by revealing some of these undesirable patterns, helping to identify their sources and to correct them. A person's posture, for example, or the way he habitually knits his brow, or clenches his jaw, may reveal significant information about inner complexes or personality problems.*

SENSATION AND THE UNCONSCIOUS

We have described the five senses as essentially a part of the function of the conscious mind. But, here also there is an interrelation with the unconscious. Have you ever been walking down a street, living, so far as you know, in the here and the now? Suddenly, for no apparent reason, you get a "flash," perhaps of a childhood scene, or some person or event of the past that you were not even consciously thinking about. Up out of some recess of your mind it came, seemingly unbidden. What happened? Perhaps,

*See "Analyzing the Feedback" in *The Elements of Effective Communication*, by W. A. Mambert, Acropolis Books, Washington, D.C., 1971.

without your even consciously realizing it, one of your senses evoked a stored memory from somewhere in your mind. You may have momentarily smelled an odor that "carried you back" to a childhood incident, or caught the flutter of a leaf or a familiar color in the corner of your eye. Here, again, what has happened is that your conscious has dipped into your unconscious, aided by your conscious senses.

Because your conscious functions such as your physical senses interact so intimately with your unconscious mind, the same kind of thing can happen while you are asleep. A change in room temperature while you sleep, for example, can project you into another season or time. A sound can trigger a whole dramatic event. While you are asleep, too, as we shall see in more detail later, your unconscious is even more active and imaginative than while you are awake, and we shall see how you can interpret some of this activity too.

CREATIVITY AND ARTISTIC EXPRESSION

These are excellent examples of how the conscious and unconscious interact. Painting a picture or sculpting in clay, presumably conscious activities, often are literal trips into the inner world of the unconscious. Many therapists use painting and modeling as a part of their analysis of patients because these activities often do reveal the unconscious through conscious activity. Frequently, the person doing the painting is just as surprised at its contents as is anyone else. Jung himself used painting to work out the contents of his own unconscious and dreams. Little actual artistic training is required to put this into practice. One can simply take pen or brush in hand and begin, letting the picture develop itself. Its content, however inept and amateur, can be interpreted.

"From nowhere, seemingly, I saw the answer to the

problem . . . in a sudden flash the picture was there in my mind," are common exclamations of the creative person. What has actually happened is that this person has tapped the hidden resources of his unconscious mind. The answer, the solution, the picture, the creation, was there all along. Its elements were "stored" somewhere within the recesses of the unconscious. They were evoked in a certain combinatory way into the conscious level and found expression through whatever expressive skill the person possessed—in the mathematician, a formula; in the painter, a picture; in the engineer, a new invention; in the child, a simplistic, primitive drawing; and so on.

PSYCHODRAMA

More and more analysts and therapists today are using psychodrama and role playing to help people work out their problems of adjustment and coping. To a large extent, these activities also involve using an interaction of the conscious and unconscious parts of the mind. In this practice, patients are encouraged to act out how they feel about certain things that are happening in their lives, things which perhaps because of some inhibition they cannot act out in the real world. When this activity is observed, it often can be translated into personal needs that are not being met in an individual's lifestyle. Corrections can be made in the pattern of living to alleviate the conflict this causes, and the person can learn to function and cope more normally. Perhaps a change in job, for example, may be indicated, or a new activity that fulfills a basic need to create or to work out aggressiveness. Henry Thoreau was so right when he said that many of us lead lives of quiet desperation, never truly fulfilling ourselves as human beings and becoming the full celebrators of life that we could and ought to be.

ACTIVE IMAGINATION

Jung grouped many conscious-unconscious activities under the general heading of what he called the *active imagination*. He saw that something other than the mere stimuli of the thinking function or the outer world was active at such times. This activity was clearly related to both the conscious and unconscious, and often quite revelatory of the deeper beings of people. He saw also that these activities had numerous characteristics in common with dreams. Both he and Dr. Freud also found that by assisting disturbed people to bring this capability into play and focus, through a process called *free association*, they could actually "dip into" the contents of people's unconscious minds and identify complexes and dysfunctions (hangups).

Application of the active imagination through free association now is used rather extensively in psychotherapy to bring the hidden, unconscious contents of people's minds out into the open where they can be dealt with. So long as something remains in the unconscious, it remains unknown to patient and therapist alike. Again, once something is at the conscious level, where it can be seen and handled, the chances of effectively dealing with and treating it increase tremendously. Usually free association involves encouraging a person to say anything that comes into his mind and then to "chain" the thoughts and impressions that follow upon it. Jung called this latter process *amplification*. This amplification process eventually can expand the original image or thought, ultimately leading to the source of a particular emotional trouble or complex. Jung also frequently used various versions of the familiar "word association test" to help his subjects more quickly focus upon specific inner conflicts. In this method, the analyst states a "trigger" word and asks the subject to respond immediately, without stopping to think about his answer, with the first word, image or thought that "pops" into his mind. The analyst then closely observes both the time it takes a person to respond and the nature of his response, thereby giving at least a preliminary idea of where certain associations might be giving a patient trouble. Used in conjunction with other observations and a full knowledge of the person's larger life and current emotional situation, such free association has proved a valuable aid in treating emotional illness.

Hopefully, the foregoing has expanded the reader's view of exactly what "conscious" really means. As can be seen, it is far more than might meet the casual eye. It involves a rather elaborate interaction of the total, conscious-unconscious being of an individual person. At least a basic understanding of this interaction is essential to any intelligent approach to understanding one's inner self. In summary, the important things to remember are:

1. "Conscious" encompasses many aspects and functions of the human mind.
2. There is no clear line of demarcation between the conscious and the unconscious.
3. The aim is always toward a harmonious existence of the two.
4. The conscious is in a continuous state of growth and change.
5. Conscious activity can give important clues and insights into the unconscious self.

3

The Personal Unconscious

Understanding your own conscious mind is not enough. For, as we are trying to show, this is only a part of your *whole* mind and self. A knowledge of the structure and function of the personal unconscious is also a part of the necessary foundation for meaningful self analysis. As already mentioned, there is considerable evidence that the unconscious is even more expansive and inclusive than the conscious. Studies of the powers of the human mind, experiments with word association tests, hypnosis, free association, observation of the conscious activities described in the foregoing chapter, and the study of dreams, substantiate this. Tests in hypnotic regression, for example, indicate that the details of incidents in a person's past life, from earliest childhood to the present, are stored somewhere beneath the conscious surface of the mind. Dreams bear this out too. For in dreaming one also is able to remember the oldest and minutest of details. Where does this data come from? Where is it stored? Somewhere within the psyche of the individual person there seems to be an

34

almost limitless repository of remembered information and experience. This we call the personal unconscious.

Labeling the unconscious as a *sub*conscious, as some psychologists do, implies that it is under or separate and apart from something; that is, from the conscious. The evidence is much stronger that it is *with* the conscious—that it exists and functions during consciousness and wakefulness, as well as during sleep, dreaming, the hypnotic state, or any other psychic suspension of conscious activity. One might say that the unconscious never sleeps or lies dormant. It is more accurate, perhaps, to say that it lies in wait.

The unconscious might be described as a kind of deep well, with its upper ranges nearer to the conscious, and successively receding downward into the deeper and darker recesses of the mind (Figure 3-1). One's more recent

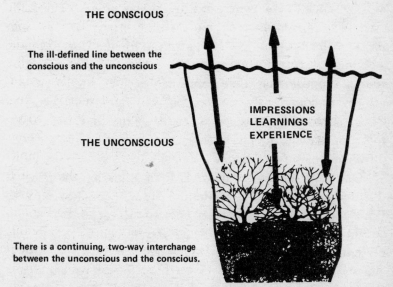

THE CONSCIOUS

The ill-defined line between the
conscious and the unconscious

IMPRESSIONS
LEARNINGS
EXPERIENCE

THE UNCONSCIOUS

There is a continuing, two-way interchange
between the unconscious and the conscious.

Figure 3-1. The human unconscious is very much like a deep well. Many experiences, impressions and learnings, both recent and past, are stored in it. Almost all of its contents are accessible and frequently come forward, regardless of how old they are. In addition, the unconscious continually exerts an influence upon conscious behavior.

experiences seem to be stored in the upper ranges nearer to the conscious level, and older experiences seem to "seep" down to the lower reaches of the psyche. There also seems to be a rather ill-defined area between the unconscious and conscious where various thoughts, feelings, impulses, and responses "bounce" into and out of the conscious and the unconscious. Nearly everyone has had the "on the tip of my tongue" experience. Some thought or idea momentarily flits though the consciousness, almost penetrates to the brain's speech center and then is lost—forgotten. Where did this thought come from? Where did it go? It was already in the mind or it would not have evidenced itself. Did it then somehow leave the mind? No: it probably came out of and receded back into the unconscious.

All of the things that a person knows or has experienced (through the senses, intuitively, rationally or emotionally), but of which he is not aware at the moment, are contained somewhere in the unconscious. This may even include things which may have been perceived without one's realizing that he has perceived them. For example, one might consciously remember having been in a certain room. Suppose that that room had a clock in it that was not even consciously noticed. If the eyes had seen the clock, the unconscious has a record of the time, and under the proper conditions that time is retrievable. This has been proven with subjects under hypnosis.

One may be quite amazed upon thinking about what the unconscious might contain. For, it seems not only to store the record of one's personal total past experience; it continues to record and make its influence felt in the present. But perhaps even more significantly, in a sense it already contains at least a part of one's psychological future, the dawning, primordial shapes of future psychic events. Because, as in almost every other observable part of nature, when certain courses of events are set into motion, when certain conditions are set up, the future results of those events and conditions, assuming that they continue uninterrupted, are often quite predictable. And the significant thing is that, if you gear yourself to listen and interpret what is going on inside of you, you can indeed often "hear," or even "see," what your own unconscious is predicting. Anything that will ever come to shape in the conscious already exists in the unconscious. Where else could it be, if it arises out of the mind?

As already mentioned, the unconscious exerts a continuing influence upon the conscious. Its contents frequently behave as if they were conscious. It contains a host of obscured experiences, impressions, feeling, images and thoughts which, despite the fact that we do not consciously "know" them, are nevertheless present and influence both our thinking and behavior. Take the person, for example, who starts to do something or perhaps to go somewhere. Suddenly he has forgotten what it is that he has intended to do. Yet, he continues in the direction of doing it. He is guided by his unconscious mind. Then he remembers what he had set out to do. It is his unconscious that has prompted him.

It is possible to see the unconscious at work, particularly in the observation of neurotic behavior. Often, this is the only way to explain the frequently totally irrational and disconnected behavior of patients in terms of both speech and action. The unconscious actually takes over and supersedes the conscious in the waking state, just as it does in the dreaming state. In a sense, the neurotic can actually live his dream. The alert and discerning physician or psychiatrist will, in fact, interpret the neurotic behavior much in the same way that a dream is interpreted and gain valuable data from it. Nor need such interpretation be restricted to the out-and-out neurotic. For neurotic symptoms also can be observed in normal people as well.

The simple truth is that the conscious mind exercises at best a tenuous control over the total psyche. Most people do not realize just how weak so-called "will power" really is.

The truth of the matter is that many of us would actually be better off if we listened to the unconscious a little more than we do—if we *got in touch* with what is clearly the greater portion of our psychic beings. We would, in most cases, be tapping a neglected resource and wellspring of useful information and capabilities. But more importantly, we would be taking a step toward becoming more aware, integrated, individuated total persons.

Another related phenomenon that illustrates the permeating nature of the unconscious and its influences over the conscious is what psychologists have come to call *cryptomnesia,* or literally "concealed recollection." This also is very similar to the American Romantic writer's idea of what Ralph Waldo Emerson called the *oversoul* and *spontaneous recollection.* We speak here of the occurrence of "trigger" events that spontaneously bring contents of the unconscious into the consciousness. Frequently, such events are caused by the senses. For example, as mentioned in the previous chapter, a certain odor recalls a whole series of events which a moment before was not present in the conscious. One enters a room for the first time and senses that he has been there before. The sight of, perhaps, a certain chair, or wallpaper, a forgotten tune, the ticking of a clock, or the velvety feeling of a drapery suddenly recalls a whole chain of *subliminal* (below the level of usual arousal) experiences and impressions hitherto "forgotten," but not really forgotten, merely stored; for the unconscious forgets nothing. Actually, it is a quite normal function of the conscious to forget in this manner. Because its job, as the modern computer operator would say, is to remain "online," in a "real-time" mode, "processing" current incoming data, coping with the here-and-now. If this did not happen, the conscious mind would become a hopelessly confused and jumbled clutter and would not be able to perform its primary waking tasks.

This concealed recollection, as Jung called it, can have several important functions in waking life, and can actually be controlled and directed toward some very pleasant experiences. Following is an excerpt of an article written by one of the authors for *Woman's Day* some years ago.

MY TIME MACHINE
by W. A. Mambert*

. . . How many times has something been right under your nose, and you couldn't see it for looking? That's the way my time machine was; it was even closer. I discovered it quite accidentally. on a rainy Saturday afternoon. I had turned wistfully from staring out of my bedroom window at the drizzle and tossed myself lazily on the bed. The whisk broom was lying where I had thrown it in a careless moment, instead of hanging it where it belonged. Aimlessly, I picked it up hefted it and, for some reason, held it to my nose and sniffed it. In less time than it takes to finish a whole sniff I found myself lolling atop a wagonload of new-cut hay, chewing on a sweet, golden shoot. My grandfather's voice filtered through to me as he hyahed the horses on through the hay dust to where another pitchfork-load was waiting to be hefted up to him. As I rolled nonchalantly out of the way, not really caring whether I was buried or not, the whole expanse of azure sky came into view, and a couple of black dots circled and swooped far above.

A pencil is good for a trip, too. Sitting at my desk, trying to think of something clever to say about a product of modern science and waiting for quitting time, I unconsciously toy with my pencil. It passes under my nose. Suddenly, I am holding a wonderfully new pencil box in my hands, proudly admiring a full half-dozen pencils. red, blue and yellow. There is an eraser. a

*W. A. Mambert, "My Time Machine," *Woman's Day*, August, 1961.

sharpener and a ruler. And they all have a smell I've never forgotten. A chain reaction starts. The big blue school bus is coming down the county road to take me to my very first day of school. I want to run back down the dirt road to the farmhouse. I don't want to go to school; but I get on just as I did the first time. It's a new bus, and it smells new. I've always remembered the smell of a new bus.

I sense that you've already gotten onto what I'm talking about. And you know that you've got the same model time machine I have. Maybe you haven't used it for a while. Why not try now? What's that by your hand? Pick it up! That's it; now sniff it. Close your eyes . . . *bon voyage*!

All of the impressions and memories recorded here were stored somewhere within the author's psyche and merely "triggered" by the simple use of one of the functions of the conscious.

WHERE DOES THE UNCONSCIOUS COME FROM?

We have already touched slightly upon this. A baby is not born with a full-fledged mind. The main contents of both the conscious and unconscious mind are cumulative. They grow with the rest of the person and his psyche as he or she grows and develops throughout life. We saw in the foregoing chapter that most (but not all) of the contents of the unconscious once were conscious. That is, they came into the mind or psyche through one of the conscious functions, namely, thinking, feeling, intuition or sensing. For one of two basic reasons, they ultimately become conscious.

The first reason, as we have mentioned, is that, for the sheer sake of efficiency, impressions, thoughts, emotions, perceptions, etc., are stored away to permit the conscious portion of the psyche to function in the present. The second reason is more significant for self-adjustment. Your psyche may also *repress* certain information—stick it on the backshelf of the mind, so to speak, because it is too painful, traumatic or troublesome to deal with. This is the dangerous part. The human mind functions in such a way that these things do not go away merely because they are ignored or shelved. The contrary is true. The longer they are repressed, the more likely are they to cause trouble. They not only continue to exist; they grow and fester, continue to try to make their presence known and to assert themselves in such activities as dreaming and as influences on our conscious waking behavior.

WHY THE "PERSONAL" UNCONSCIOUS

The term *personal* unconscious is used to distinguish a very important distinction about the overall human unconscious. More seems to be stored within the human mind than that which can be explained in terms of the personal experience which that mind has had. There is some evidence that *everything* in the unconscious was not once conscious. C. G. Jung believed a part of the unconscious may come into the world with a person when he or she is born. He called this inherited portion the *collective unconscious*. That is, there seems to be a part of the unconscious that is not acquired in this life. This may be of particular importance to the interpretation of certain types of dreams, which Jung called *archetypal* dreams. These ideas are explained more fully later. For the moment, it is sufficient to know that there may be something within the total human unconscious other than one's personal experience as an individual person. The idea is not new that there is something that binds each of us to all other humans who are living with us now and who have lived before us in the past—and which will link us psychically to all who inhabit this earth after we are gone. Nor is it beyond the realm of possibility that there is a higher level of consciousness or unconsciousness above or beyond the personal level—something that enables us to communicate outside of the verbal range. Some mystics refer to this idea in the term *superconscious*, which relates to such phenomena as extra-sensory perception, clairvoyance, etc. These are areas in which serious scientific observation is just beginning, although the ancients explored them quite extensively. We shall look at these also in a later chapter to see how they relate to the subject of total personal adjustment.

A WISER PERSON INSIDE

As already pointed out, the unconscious portions of our psyches are not clear-cut parts separate and distinct from the conscious portions. What you really are observing is a single whole, a conscious-unconscious mind that functions as an integrated mechanism. The unconscious, in other words, is of the same "stuff" as the conscious. It has all of the functions of the conscious. In addition to being a storage place for information and experience, it also thinks and rationalizes. In fact, as many ancient writers surmised, it now has been almost definitely established that the thinking and evaluating powers of the unconscious exceed those of the conscious. The reason for this is a simple one. Recall that the unconscious has, so far as is known, an infinite capacity for remembering. This means that it also remembers all of the best and most logical ways of doing things that its possessor has been exposed to (remember, the wrong ways of doing things are also stored). As an example, suppose that you are exposed to a sure-fire method of committing the perfect crime. Strategically, logically and rationally there is no possible way of getting caught. Suppose even further that in certain circles this crime would not even be considered to be wrong. That is, extenuating circumstances actually may justify the act at the conscious level. You might even, therefore, consider at the conscious level that you actually are performing someone a service, or acting morally. There are many situations in today's complex life such as this. At the conscious level, there is no problem with the act. However, stored deep within your unconscious may be an entirely different rationale of a higher morality. Also within that unconscious is a capability for perceiving the true realities of a situation unclouded by all of the ramifications of the outer world. In short, most of the time, there is a much wiser person inside you than the conscious one who walks around in this world, often impulsive, easily confused, easily convinced and capable of rationalizing almost anything that it wants to do. A dream recently told to us by a successful young businessman illustrates this point.

> I was with three people whose faces I could not distinguish. Yet, I was aware that two of them seemed to be in basic agreement with me. We were planning to go to a nearby city to commit a robbery. It was the second time that we were going to do this. I clearly saw our plan, the route we would take, and actually, in the dream, was able to project myself into the future and see us performing the robbery. Simultaneously, as I was in the future situation in the dream, watching us in action—and *getting caught*—the third person in our planning group was voicing a warning that things would not go as smoothly this time as they had on the first job. Something would go wrong, and we would be caught.

We engaged in several rather lengthy conversations with this person before obtaining a clue as to what the meaning of this dream might be. He seemed to be an ethical person. He lived a normal life, had never actually committed a crime of any kind, and could not conceive of himself doing so. Yet, in his dream he had done so and was planning to do it again. Quite by accident one day, actually outside the counseling situation, the interpretation of this dream thrust itself upon us. He was telling us at lunch about how well things were going for him in business and that he soon would be able to make a sizable contribution to our church. It seemed that his company had just made a rather large sale to a local government organization. The head of the government agency who had authorized the procurement and signed the contract, and with whom Jim had become quite friendly since the sales negotiations had begun some months ago, had approached him with a very attractive proposition for setting up a "little company" on the side to perform maintenance services on the equipment which the agency had ordered. For certain services, Jim was to receive stock in the company, as well as a very attractive "retainer." Quite familiar with the workings of what he euphemistically called "symbiotic relationships," Jim had been pondering the deal for a couple of weeks, and had convinced himself that his was a clear-cut situation, with no conflict of interests involved. He knew, however, that his company did have a subsidiary maintenance company. In the absence of any other situation in his life, so far as we could determine, to which the dream might apply, we concluded that the dream had some reference to this. We shall show more fully in succeeding chapters who or what the figures in this dream may have represented. For the moment, we are interested only in its overall message as an illustration of the reasoning powers of the unconscious. To us, it was clear that although Jim's conscious mind saw nothing wrong with the deal, or at least had rationalized that there was nothing wrong, his inner reasoning powers were telling him something different. His latent sense of morality, if you will, residing deeper within his psyche, first of all told Jim that he had "been this route before." Somewhere, at some time, it had learned to distinguish the finer nuances of right and wrong. To Jim's unconscious, he was in effect committing a robbery; it used the robbery as a *symbol* for what he was doing.

A FLASH OF GENIUS

As mentioned in the foregoing chapter, studies of human creativity have revealed another important resource of the unconscious as more than a mere depository of events of the past. For not only do older contents recede into it; totally new contents emerge from it. That is, the unconscious seems to have the ability to *create*, to combine its contents into totally new thoughts and creative ideas that were never before a part of the conscious mind. There are a great many cases on record to substantiate this thesis, especially among artists, writers and similar creative people. The nineteenth century German philosopher Kekule, for example, asserted that the molecular structure of benzene was revealed to him in a dream. Rene Descartes, the great French philosopher, asserted that a "mystical revelation" revealed to him in a flash the "order of all the sciences." Robert Louis Stevenson asserted that he had searched for years for a story plot that would reveal the duality and coexistence of good and evil in man. The plot for *Dr. Jekyl and Mr. Hyde* was revealed to him in a dream. Edgar Allan Poe, the father of the American mystery thriller, attributed the ideas for many of his yet unequalled suspense stories to ideas that arose "spontaneously" from somewhere within him.

In a recent paper entitled "The Flash of Genius," Alfred B. Barret of Ohio State University reports his research on the creative work involved in several important modern scientific studies. He relates in some detail how these creative discoveries evolved out of the mental data bases of their discoverers. Following are the actual case studies he made:

Sir Ernest Rutherford and the Nuclear Atom

Roy J. Plunkett and Teflon

W. C. Roentgen and X-rays

Thomas Midgley and Albert L. Henne and Freon
Midgley, Boyd and Hochualt and Lead Tetraethyl
C. M. Hall and Electrolytic Aluminum Processing
Giaugue and Johnston and The Discovery of Radioactive Isotopes
Henri Beguerel and Radioactivity
Niels Bohr and The Bohr Atomic Model
Sir James Chadwick and Identification of the Neutron
George de Hevesy and Radioactive Tracers

Each of these people reported that his discovery emanated from or related in some way to the "sudden flash," the illuminating or revelatory experience from the inner contents of the mind. Such ability to create is within all of us in varying degrees. It usually is merely a case of how willing we are, as St. Augustine put it, to "submit to the new sensation and refreshment."

AN EXPERIENCE WITH YOUR UNCONSCIOUS

You may wish at this time to test your own unconscious. This is easy to do. Try this experiment. First, read all seven steps; follow their suggestions on the second reading.

1. What are you thinking of right now, as you read?
2. Stop for a moment.
3. Think of your mother (or any other person you have known).
4. Let your mind ponder the thought for a moment.
5. Develop a mental image of this person.
6. Now, for about five minutes, let your mind wander where it will. Do not try to control the thoughts and images that come.
7. Do not read any further for the moment. Close your eyes and look away from the page.

Did you experience thoughts and feelings that you were not experiencing a moment ago? If you did, what happened was that through the "trigger mechanism" we suggested to you, you were able to evoke images and memories which a moment before were stored in another, hidden part of your mind.

Try another experiment, looking away from the page and closing your eyes as you do so. First, think of a shape or an object, perhaps a circle or a square. Now concentrate on that shape. Form an image of it in your mind and watch that image. Again, do not attempt to control what you see. Merely let it exist and be, move and develop with a "will" of its own. Just watch and observe what it does or becomes. Do this for about five minutes and then return to the page.

If you "cooperated" with your mental imagery, you have just experienced the existence and operation of your unconscious. These experiments are known as free association or what Jung called active imagination. At the very least, they show that there is, in fact, a realm within you beyond, beneath or throughout that which you are consciously experiencing or knowing at the moment. This is your unconscious.

OUR MANY SELVES

Among the most important things that one must understand in order to intelligently and realistically interpret dreams is the psychological phenomenon which Jung called *complex*. Almost all people have some complexes within their unconscious. Basically, a complex is a grouping of associated ideas, feelings and psychological responses that a person's mind sets up in order for him to deal with certain life situations. The complex, in effect, is a psychic energy force within the unconscious. Complexes usually are highly charged with emotion and are of an unpleasant or painful character. They usually build up over a relatively long period of time within a person's life, frequently beginning in childhood, although they also can form rather quickly as a result of a traumatic experience.

Most of the time, complexes are wholly or partially repressed into the unconscious; that is, they are not as likely to be known to the conscious mind. It is their results and influences upon the personality that are more likely to be known. For example, claustrophobia, the fear of being confined or closed in, could be classed as a complex. The person with the fear knows that he has it, but he may or may not be aware of the associations within his unconscious that cause it. When one analyzes the nature of a complex such as this, it becomes apparent that what it really is is a behavior pattern that has been set up within the mind in order to deal with an undesirable or intolerable set of circumstances in life. Such complexes can exert their influence upon both conscious and unconscious behavior. Many times, they are stronger than the conscious will and succeed in taking over the behavior of the person, in effect, overriding his reason or what he wants to do.

One of these behavior patterns that we call complexes is what many psychologists call the *Oedipus complex*, which sheds light on the nature of complexes in general. In Greek mythology, Oedipus unknowingly killed his own father, Laius, King of Thebes. Oedipus appears in various plays by the Greek dramatist Sophocles (496-406). The Oedipus complex refers to an abnormal attachment of a son to a mother and a corresponding hate or hostility for the father. This is usually associated with guilt and emotional conflict on the part of the son. The name comes from the fact that Oedipus later discovered that he had killed his own father, married his mother, and was burdened with guilt over the fact. The Oedipus complex might be called a specialized form of the familiar "guilt complex," that is, the feeling of guilt is the means by which the person's psyche deals with the painful situation.

The feminine opposite of the Oedipus complex is the *Electra complex*, which refers to an abnormal attachment of a daughter to a father and corresponding hostility to the mother. In the post-Homeric legends of the Greeks, Electra urged her brother Orestes to kill their mother.

Many complexes, or whatever one chooses to call these behavior patterns, build up in childhood, are continually repressed by an individual, remain beneath the surface in adulthood, and usually cause considerable trouble and agony if they are not brought out into the open and dealt with. Psychoanalysts who deal in dream interpretation see complexes as very important. For in dreams one can often see these complexes more clearly. Thus, the chances of exposing and dealing with them are great. One of the most interesting and revealing aspects of complexes is that they often seem to *behave as separate personalities against the will or knowledge of the person in whom they exist*. This may be what compelled St. Paul to utter "The good that I would, I do not; and that which I would not, I do." Because of their tendency to behave as separate or "splinter" personalities—and because of the symbolic nature of dreams—*complexes may often actually become personified in dreams*. They may appear as people with easily described characteristics; for example, a mischievous child, a pouting, "bitchy" female, a frightfully dark and evil or ugly person, or a benevolent and benign person. The variations are many. There are "many selves" within each of us, all seeking to be heard, to have their say-so, to obtain their share of the living that the body and psyche in which they exist are engaged.

The idea of the complex fits into the ideas of wholeness and individuation in a couple of significant ways. Most people think of the complex as *abnormal* behavior. In actuality, it is most often not. Jung demonstrated that it is merely an *overdevelopment* of a quite natural part of the human personality. Take the so-called *inferiority complex*, for example. All children start out in life with a natural feeling of helplessness, ineffectiveness and weakness. In normal development, this would be outgrown and substituted by a balanced sense of one's self, worth, and rightful place in the scheme of things. In many of us, however, what happens is that the basic tendency may be reinforced in a variety of ways that inhibit the normal development. The influences that cause this may vary greatly. For example, unequal economic opportunity, health defects, constant criticism in childhood, or even a missing parent, may perpetuate the basic feeling of unequalness or inferiority.

Once such a developmental cycle begins, it is very difficult to overcome. Gradually, as the person grows to maturity, even those circumstances that do not really indicate that he is inferior are interpreted by his psyche as such and continue to reinforce the complex. As one sees others around him presumably superior to him (although within they are quite likely to have the same feelings he has), this becomes quite painful and unacceptable to him. He therefore represses the feelings, pushes them farther and farther into his unconscious where, as Jung put it, they tend to "group" and form "little personalities unto themselves."

This splinter personality or complex, however, still continues to make its presence known and to try to equalize the situation. It seeks to control and have a share of the conscious world by causing the individual to behave, as Alfred Adler, another famous modern psychologist put it, in a compensatory way. Probably this is why people with inferiority complexes sometimes behave in a superior way. To relieve the fears and frustrations associated with real or imagined inferiorities in the past, the unconscious exaggerates the opposite feeling—of self-importance and self-value—as a defensive mechanism. There is, among other things, a pronounced effort to achieve, to excel, and to obtain the recognition of others. Interestingly, there is a paradox here. For it often is a feeling of inferiority, and the behavioral complex that results from it, which is responsible for genuinely superior accomplishment. But the tragedy, in terms of individual adjustment, is that usually the possessor of the complex cannot let go of his compulsive behavior even *after* he has proved to himself and the world that he is just as good as or better than anyone else. His complex is too deeply ingrained. His frustrations therefore continue. He remains essentially an unhappy, discontented, even miserable person, unable to rest, relax, or let up in his continual, compulsive, inner struggle to overcome that deep, personal sense that he still is and may never be as good as anyone else.

Inferiority, excessive mother-love and father-hostility, excessive father love and mother-hostility, of course, are not the only complexes. They are merely among the most common and easily identified ones. It will be found, however, that many other internal, compulsive behavior patterns do in some way usually tie or relate to these. For, if you stop and think about it, there are only a very few basic relationships among people in this world. And it is our internal interpretation of our relationship to the outer world and the people in it that determines most of our adjustment to that world and its contents.

Nevertheless, each of us has his own hidden complexes or other selves—the ugly, the dark, the foolish, the suspicious, the inferior. But we also have *good complexes* which may be, and often are, equally hidden and repressed—the beautiful, the benevolent, the profound. These too may be seeking to assert and express themselves. Strangely, the world can be equally cruel and repressive toward these latter splinter personalities. For it is partially made up of people whose negative, defensive, compensatory feelings cause them to "put us down" when we do behave in a genuinely superior and noble way. Soon, we learn to be careful, not to expose our tender, noble feelings and impulses to just anyone. Thus, they also become repressed and hidden, venturing out into the light of day only when there is safety and security for them in perhaps a long-established relationship of trust with another individual, or in a dream. There is a risk involved in living as a full, balanced person, letting all sides of one's personality live in the open. Few of us are willing to take that risk—to live the agonies as well as the ecstasies.

Writers, poets and philosophers have pondered the perplexities and enigmas of this fundamental human paradox for many centuries. No one has ever come up with a sure-fire way for avoiding it. But thinkers have repeatedly found and expressed the certain fact that it is compatible and reconcilable *within the self*. William James calls this the "greatest discovery of our generation." It may well be that this is the only answer. Or, it may well be, as the authors of this book believe it to be, that if enough people think rightly in their hearts, the effect will be cumulative, and that society as a whole will "think right."

The only complete certainty of the moment, and the one with which we are primarily concerned in this book, is that *you*, the reader, can attain this adjustment at the personal level. You can be free. For we already know that when a person learns to free himself from the inhibitions and compulsions caused by his erroneous interpretations of the world around him, he begins to be able to live a contented, productive life. When one learns to live in harmony with his "many selves," one becomes their master instead of their slave. In the words of Jesus, "You shall know the truth, and the truth shall make you free."

One, however, cannot be free until one identifies that

from which he wishes to be free. It is in this respect that interpretation of unconscious mental activity becomes of great value. It enables one to identify those inner, shadow selves, to examine them, to see them for what they really are—to bring them out into the open where they can be given their just recompense.

FIGURES IN THE UNCONSCIOUS

We have already suggested that our many selves, those separate personalities that exist within each of us, frequently manifest themselves as actual characters or *figures* in our dreams. The unconscious also may use visual symbols instead of words to express itself, as in dreams. As many psychoanalysts have pointed out, it does not really matter how one labels these various essences that exist within each of us. The important things are to identify them, to recognize them for what they are, and to deal with them in a realistic way.

Jung identified at least four sets of responses that seem to exist in the unconscious and to manifest themselves as specific figures, especially in dreams. That is, the unconscious *structures* certain of its contents into actual figures or symbolic characters. Interestingly, if you stop and think about it, you will realize that the conscious "you" always is present in your dreams, almost always as what the novelist would call the "omniscience" or "stream of consciousness." This "you" is the Dante being conducted through Hell, Purgatory and Paradise. It is the Dr. Faustus being conducted on his tour by Mephistopheles. It also is the most real and least fictionalized or dramatized character in almost all dreams. In actuality, the other characters are just as real. It is merely that you do not recognize them as easily. Most of them are merely the other parts of you—your other selves.

Jung grouped the symbolic character groupings within

the unconscious, which identifiably structure themselves as figures in our dreams, as follows:

1. The Shadow Figure (s)
2. The Persona (s)
3. The Anima
4. The Animus

We remind you again that the labels one uses to identify these things are not nearly so important as knowing what they represent as activities and processes within one's own unconscious self. Among other things, this understanding forms the primary basis for understanding the symbolic language of dreams and the contents of specific dreams, which we shall discuss later. We have already seen the definitive basis for the shadow figure. It is basically a symbolic representation of either a complex or an underdeveloped aspect of the personality. A generalized definition of the other three will suffice for the moment. The *personas* are basically the built-up aspects of a person's personality that he shows to the outer world. The *anima* is the feminine aspect of the male personality. And the *animus* is the male aspect of the female personality. We shall see the importance of these figures as we progress. Do not worry if you do not fully understand them at this time.

You must also remember that your unconscious is not bound by the same rules of literalness that your conscious lives by. Your unconscious has a much freer range. Most of the conscious things now competing with it are "shut off" when you are asleep. This includes the necessity for logic, causal sequence and conventionality. In your unconscious mind and while you are asleep you are free from the socially-imposed necessities of being consistent, defending your ego, or conforming in any consistent way to what your socialized sense tells you is logical, right, wrong or ought to be.

A major difference between your conscious and unconscious is that your unconscious simply does not "care" about such things as logic, time and spatial relationships, the laws of waking reality or any kind of conformity. Sleep releases you from these needs, and your mind is free to range where it wishes or compels itself to go. You are free from competing with anyone or anything, from the constant battle for survival, from the thoughts and feelings that respond to challenge and the necessity to master your environment. You simply *are*. There is no need to justify the fact. In the unconscious and in sleep, "I am" is the only point of reference. It is a totally self experience. Your self says, "I dream, therefore I am," and this is sufficient.

The "you" observing the inner, unconscious drama such as in a dream, still functioning in its literal, nonsymbolic mode, can easily be confused by the lack of logical sequence and the imagery and symbology portrayed in and by the unconscious. At this point, it will help to interpret a dream reported to us by a young husband:

> I dreamed that I was walking down a road. I then was suddenly walking along the edge of a very steep precipice. As I walked and then started to run, someone kept trying to push me over the edge. Finally, he succeeded. Then I was falling. As I fell, a flock of birds kept attacking me. I saw huge, dark, jagged rocks below. As they came closer, I screamed. Then I awoke.

Interpretation of this dream will illustrate several of the points just discussed. It is important to maintain a total perspective. We must know something about this young man's larger life as well as his current conscious situation. In fact, when we know something of his past and current life situation, much of the interpretation automatically comes clear. At the time of the dream, John was thirty-two and had been married for thirteen years. He and his wife had four children. As we counseled with him, we found that since childhood, until a year or so ago, he had been a regular church goer, a faithful family man, and believed rather strongly in the morals taught by the church. He had been raised in this way by his parents and had continued in his standards of thinking when he had established his own family. A year ago, he had begun to have an affair with a young woman and was still seeing her at the time he had the dream. Several days before the dream he had thought that he had caught a fleeting glimpse of his wife in a shopping center while he was with the girl—a "close call," as he put it. In fact, for the past year he had walked pretty much on the verge of being found out in his affair. He also felt guilty since he knew that he was committing adultery and believed it to be wrong.

Almost literally, then, he had been walking on the edge of a cliff, just as he had done in his dream. He knew, too, that if he were found out, his marriage would "go on the rocks," since his wife often had told him that she never could live with a man if he was unfaithful. In his conscious mind, however, he had been able to rationalize his relationship with the girl, and they frequently had discussed in the usual way that "anything that seemed so good and right could not possibly be bad." In other words, a part of him continued to propel him into and to perpetuate the affair.

Now let us look at the content of the dream against these psychic conditions. His own self, of course, is the audience, the main player, the omniscience and the story teller, in the drama that his unconscious has played out for him. There is another person, although he is not identifiable. Who could it be that is trying to push him over the edge? It is none other than a darker side of himself. It is what Jung called a shadow figure, representing another facet or set of responses within his psyche or personality. He cannot see the face or identify the figure because he probably does not *want* to. At the conscious level—but *only* at the conscious level—he has rationalized the darker side of himself away. His unconscious does not forget and will not permit this darker side to simply disappear. Neither has his unconscious forgotten his former standards of morality. It knows and recognizes both the "good" and "bad" sides of him. Its powers of reasoning also have not been diminished.

A good interpretation of this dream would be that his unconscious has put all of the elements of the situation together, "reasoned" them out, and concluded that if the present course of events continues, if he continues to walk along the edge of this precipice, that destructive part of his personality that causes him to do so will indeed push him over. In actuality, with the possible exception of the birds, there isn't very much obscure symbology involved in this dream. Birds have, however, been a relatively consistent element in many recorded dreams, and most frequently have represented such things as "spirits," thoughts (fleeting, swift, on the wings of thoughts, etc.), and children. Although they could represent other things, such as all of the thoughts he has had about these matters, it is much more likely that the birds represent his children here, primarily because of their immediacy to the situation. They are "attacking" him in the sense that their existence and role in his life are a part of the perplexity and conflict he is experiencing.

Interestingly, we also had an opportunity to analyze a dream of the wife, which occurred within a week of the husband's. It turned out, incidentally, that she had momentarily thought that she had seen him with a young woman. She had consciously dismissed the occurrence, but admitted in counseling that she had had a growing suspicion that things were not as they should be. She had dreamed that their home had been destroyed by fire and that her husband had been killed. Fire has been found to consistently symbolize death and sexual intercourse. In its generalized, more or less universal symbolic means, it can be interpreted as signifying such things as cleansing or destructiveness and may indicate a desire or fear of either. The wife's unconscious, therefore, seems to have had a premonition (based perhaps on evidence that her conscious chose to ignore or repress) of an impending disaster. Her dream told her symbolically that something was destroying her home and "killing" her husband or their relationship. Thanks at least partially to the counseling sessions in which the dreams were revealed, the disaster was averted and the marriage was not destroyed nor did it "go on the rocks."

This example was not particularly difficult to interpret when the personal conditions under which it occurred became known. It illustrates how the reasoning powers of the unconscious may frequently excel those of the conscious. The unconscious knows and considers that which the consciousness ignores or represses. This example also shows something of the nature of the symbolic language in which the unconscious may speak and how it may construct shadow figures to represent aspects of the personality and their messages.

CONFRONTING YOUR UNCONSCIOUS

If you have not yet begun to look into your own unconscious, you have been and still are living a partial, superficial, surface existence. This is not an accusation; it is a simple statement of fact. For the following facts remain true:

1. Your unconscious exists. It is real.
2. Your unconscious is wider, deeper and larger than your conscious world.
3. Your unconscious transcends your conscious and

exerts a continuing, powerful influence upon your whole self.

4. Your unconscious will not "go away" if it is ignored. On the contrary, its influence in all probability will grow.

So long as you do not acknowledge the existence and influence of your unconscious, you will remain almost totally at its mercy. This is precisely the condition of many people in our world today. It is the condition which, more than any other single circumstance, is responsible for the malaise of the day. More than any other factor, our individual inability to become involved with our total selves is the source of our troubles. This inability alone fills more doctors' and psychiatrists' offices, more correctional institutions, more pastoral counseling appointment books, than all other causes of personal ills and troubles combined. Nor do we speak here only of emotional troubles and ailments. Many physical illnesses actually seem to have an initial source or base in some form of this same fundamental inability in a person to reconcile his unconscious and conscious worlds.

The unconscious as a clinical concept and basis for treatment was introduced over seventy-five years ago. The principles involved have been recognized by some even longer—for centuries. Yet, paradoxically, as our scientific knowledge of the physical world has grown, our insights into our inner selves seems to have diminished. Man has come to understand the structure of the atom and the whole outer physical universe. But in so doing he has dehumanized himself. He has lost his identity and become isolated from his *own being*. He has become a pitiful, drifting, disconnected particle in the very cosmos that he presumes to understand so well—but really doesn't understand at all. To modern man, you and me, the Augustinian theorem, "I think, therefore God is," has become meaningless. One cannot help repondering the ancient words of Jesus: "What shall it profit a man if he shall gain the whole world and lose his own soul?"

But what can one do? To the authors, the answer seems to spring from this page. Hopefully, it will for the reader too. The first step is to *acknowledge your unconscious*. We do not mean to simply say, "All right. I acknowledge my unconscious." We mean that it must become an actual accepted fact for you. You look at your own left hand. You touch it with your right. The sensations you receive are communicated into your being. You *know* that this hand is not only a part of you—it is you. When it touches something, *you* touch something. When it feels pain, *you* feel pain. When it touches the wispy hair of a loved child, or of a loved man, or of a loved woman, *you* love and emote and know. So can, and *must*, it be with you and your unconscious self.

So what we are speaking of is your embracing of your own psyche—the essential *getting back in touch*. As we have said, your first confrontation with this other part of yourself in all probability will be painful; there will be a "psychic shock." But a positive change will almost immediately occur. There will be a noticeable relaxing or lightening of inner tension even before you begin to know specific inner details. You will no longer be exerting the energy or force necessary to maintain the barrier between your conscious and your unconscious.

Gradually, then, you also will experience what is best described as an expanding consciousness. And you won't, incidentally, need any drugs or other material to do it. The reason for this is simple: your conscious *will* be expanding. You literally *will know more*. You will be correcting the lopsidedness of your conscious life through the increased interaction of your conscious and unconscious.

Perhaps the most interesting phenomenon that you can

feel, as you get to know your inner self, will be the wonderful sense of openness and receptivity that ensues. And with this openness will come a noticeable diminishing of undefined fear and anxiety. You will come to the realization that the inner tautness so common to all of us has been, in fact, fear—fear of self—fear of our many selves.

We would not have you believe, however, that all will be easy, nor that the same old urges to shut out the unconscious will not continue. Man simply is not constructed that way. The process of individuation, of becoming whole and self-reconciled, is a continuing one. It will continue throughout your life. The fulfillments along the way are actually the real payoff. Man functions with a design and a goal. The goal is individuation, which may never be fully attained. The design is the day-by-day striving toward that goal. The adventure of *becoming* is the fulfillment. The actual victory is in the combination of knowing the goal and the striving toward it and not, as some might think, only in the final attainment viewed in retrospect. Success, in other words, is in the *living*, not in the attainment. There is sufficient living available to all of us. We do not have to wait to live.

The Cardinal rose with a dignified look,
He call'd for his candle, his bell, and his book!
In holy anger, and pious grief,
He solemnly cursed that rascally thief!
He cursed him at board, he cursed him in bed;
From the sole of his foot to the crown of his head;
He cursed him in sleeping, that every night
He should dream of the devil, and wake in a fright!

Richard Harris Barham (1788-1845)
Ingoldsby Legends. The Jackdaw of Rheims.

4
A Doorway to Your Unconscious

How can the average person, who probably has little or no psychoanalytical training, gain access to the contents of his or her own unconscious? One of the best ways to do this is through your own dreams. We do not speak here of dream interpretation as a parlor game, but as a serious attempt to discover what is going on in the deeper parts of your self, your unconscious, as a basis for a fuller self-knowledge. When you understand what they are and approach their contents in an intelligent way as real events in your total psychic makeup, your dreams present the most available and most convenient entry into your own unconscious. They also represent the largest body of information about your own unconscious that is directly available to you. They are the actual "stuff" and currency of this inner world of self.

YOUR DREAMS ARE REAL

Accept first that your dreams are real. They are events that actually happen in your life. Anything that happens is a part of reality. Today's "scientific-minded" thinker tends to have too limited a view of what reality includes. He is much more likely than his forebears were to confine his definition and view of reality to the physical and sensory world, to only those things that can be experienced through the five senses, measured, weighed, or viewed through a telescope or a microscope. To most of us, unless we have given the matter special study, or have reason to become consciously disturbed by particular dreams, our dreams are essentially unreal. They belong to another world. They have no bearing upon our waking hours, which is what we call our real world. What we are actually doing when we relegate our dreams to this unimportant position, however, is ignoring a large part of reality. We put ourselves out of touch with things as they *really* are, inside of us. By so doing, we greatly diminish our capabilities not only to deal with life but to experience its full potentialities as well.

If you stop and think for a moment, you will see how and why your dreams are not only real, but are an important and significant part of your total being. Assuming an average lifespan of seventy years, which, thanks to modern science, you can reasonably hope to spend on this earth, you will spend almost twenty-three years sleeping, and much of that time dreaming. You will live almost a third of your life in what amounts to another world. Anyone who spends twenty-three years doing anything ought to take a look at what he is doing during that time.

There is another consideration that indicates that dreams have importance as a part of our total being. So far in his exploration of both his inner and outer worlds, man has definitely been able to observe at least one very consistent phenomenon. This is that there is a great deal of order and structure in both realms. Everything observed seems to fit in some way into a larger whole. Nor do things merely fit in a static or passive way. Very little seems to happen by accident or chance. In all of life, things perform some function. That is, they contribute to the existence, performance, or survival of whatever they are a part of. This phenomenon of order and purpose has been self-evident ever since man began to think. It has, in fact, become a taken-for-granted presupposition. Nobody even bothers to question it any more. The question for the modern thinker rarely if ever is: Does this or that phenomenon *have* a purpose? It always is: *What* is the purpose? There is no reason to suppose that the world of sleep and dreaming does not also fit into the larger, purposeful, functional scheme of things. On the contrary, thanks largely to the work of psychiatrists such as Jung and Freud, there is much reason to suppose that dreams do have significance, meaning and purposes in the overall structure of our lives.

In many ways, the modern researcher in psychiatry merely confirms and expands upon what has been known or suspected about the nature of man for many centuries. For example, the idea of an intangible, nonmaterial part of man's being, beyond or beneath his sensory and conscious existence, has been around since the earliest days that man first began to examine his own being. Such ideas as the duality of man, even the multiplicity within him, his fundamental drives and cravings, his needs, his inner conflicts, etc., have been expounded upon by sensitive thinkers for centuries. Some of these earlier thinkers, in fact, seemed to be in closer touch with their total selves than we are. Technological man is notoriously out of touch with himself. He has forgotten how to be a total person. It might even be possible that he could learn something from his predecessors. In the Upanishads of the ancient books of India, for example, predating the birth of Buddha in the fifth century B.C., one reads:

> Ganaka Vaideha said: "When the sun and moon have gone down, I Yagnavalkya, and the fire has gone out, and there is no sound, where is the light of man?
> Yagnavalkya said: "The self is the light."
> Ganaka Vaideha said: "Who is the Self?"
> Yagnavalkya answered: "He who is in the heart, a person of light and of knowledge, remaining the same, roams between the two worlds. As man dreams, he transcends this world and the ways of death. There are two states in man, one in this world, the second in the other world, and there is a third state between, sleep and dream. In dreaming, man sees both worlds together. He sees both evil and good. In this state, he is self-illuminated. There are no real chariots, or horses, or roads, or joys, no lakes or rivers. He is the maker of these . . . Going to and fro in his dream, the God shapes himself in man's ways, both rejoicing and seeing frightful things . . . Therefore it is said, Do not awaken a man suddenly, lest he does not get rightfully back into his body . . . This indeed is his real form."

Many such early passages illustrate the continuing concern and the "intouchness" of earlier man with the reality of the activity of his inner being. This thinker clearly saw that the inner workings of the self are a real part of the whole person. Although his language may be archaic, much of the thought is as modern as if it had been written yesterday. Even the idea about a man "not getting rightfully back into his own body," expressed in the modern psychiatric terms of perhaps a "split personality" (a separation from self and reality), is not entirely inaccurate.

Some of the best-known examples of earlier man's contact with his inner self are found in the Bible, for example, in the tales of the dreams of King Nebuchadnezzar and their interpretation by Daniel; of the dreams of Joseph and Pharaoh, and of course in the story of the dreams surrounding the birth of Jesus in the New Testament. The Jewish Talmud, which covers a period of philosophical and religious thought development of some five hundred years, from the first century B.C. to near the end of the fifth century, gives a most detailed account of the prescribed method of dream interpretation. This writing states that Jerusalem had official dream interpreters. Rabbi Chisda, one of the writers, states almost exactly what modern psychoanalysts would say many centuries later—that uninterpreted dreams are like unread letters. "They are," he said, "the messages of our inner light and understanding to our outer selves."

Aristotle (384-322 B.C.), the greatest of all Greek scientists, acknowledged creator of the science of logic and reason, also anticipated much modern psychiatric theory. He made the correct assumption, for example, that during sleep we are frequently more logical and rational than while awake. Another thinker of the Classical Period, Lucretius of Rome, anticipated the modern theory of dreams as a form of wish-fulfillment, that is, living through in our sleep the things that we could not, would not, or would like to do while awake. In both Indian and Greek culture, dream interpretation was (and still is) used in the diagnosis of illness. This is particularly interesting in the light of what we know today about psychosomatic illnesses (*psyche* is the original Greek word for "soul"; *soma* is the Greek root for body)—diseases brought about by the interaction of soul (today, mind) and body. Modern psychoanalysts seem to agree that our unconscious is often much more intimately connected and attuned to what is going on "inside us" than our conscious mind may be. All of these workings are not fully understood today. But, from what is known, an intimate relationship between our psyches and our bodies is definitely indicated. Your deep unconscious and your conscious are all part of the same mind, the same psyche, the same soul, dwelling in a single body. And, though we do not yet understand the full nature of the "language" in which they speak to each other, speak they do.

St. Augustine who stood at the crossroads of the period of classical antiquity and medieval thought, carried forth the traditional views, intermingled with the new Christian cosmology also sweeping the world at the time of the fall of Rome (476 A.D.). The powers of the mind, said Augustine, are not diminished by sleep. Sleep merely dulls the corporeal senses and the soul submits with pleasure to the new sensation and refreshment. Yet sleep does not remove the powers of sensing and thinking. For the mind still sees images of things seen in waking of such similarity to sensible things that they cannot be distinguished from those things of which they are images. If the mind thinks anything, said Augustine, it is as true in sleeping as in waking. For, as an example, he says, if the mind should argue with itself in a dream and learn something, the same principle remains immutable in wakefulness, although other aspects may be found to be false, such as the place where the argument was dreamed to have occurred, or if persons in the dream were only imagined beings. In other words, places, people, and events could be symbolic. Augustine correctly anticipated what we now accept: that dreams speak in a language of their own, a language of symbols.

A LEGACY OF FEAR

One of the problems in modern man's acceptance of the significance of his dreams and the validity of their interpretation stems from his overreaction to the unscientific thinking of his forebears. During the Middle Ages for example, the general intellectual flavor was one of superstition and overconcentration on the supernatural, into which the more occult and fearsome ideas of dream interpretation readily fitted. Many a man and woman were put to death at the stake for what they were forced to confess they had done only during their dreams. Others were executed because of their presumed influence over the dreams of others through witchcraft. Occasionally, saner voices were heard, but on the whole, superstition reigned supreme, and its results contributed much to the modern mind's general repudiation of the significance of dreams. The scientific era still reacts in extreme to the otherworldliness of the Middle Ages.

Almost all of the philosophical thinkers of the Middle Ages contributed in one way or another to our modern intellectual stereotypes about the unconscious and dreams—that curious mixture of blind faith and scientific inquiry that inhibits our acceptance of these things as part of reality and keeps us out of touch with our inner selves. Belief in demonology, possession with evil spirits, witchcraft, divine revelation, etc., more often than not were taken for granted and curiously intermingled with a kind of pseudo-scientific approach to the mind. This is quite natural and to be expected as man attempted to lift his own mind up out of the depths of superstition, to discover himself and to see the true nature of things. Many of these thinkers walked the thin line between social approval and themselves being accused of heresy or witchcraft. And, were they to be caught in an open flaunting of traditional dogma and belief, it was not unlikely that their very dreams would condemn them. For it was widely thought that demons and spirits still roamed abroad, possessing men and their minds while asleep or awake.

The development of the practice of medicine, along with its psychiatric branch, including dream interpretation, suffered similar pangs under the admixture of faith and reason. Like the philosophers, many doctors (usually laymen, and themselves often philosophers and diviners) suffered heretics' fates as they attempted to reconcile faith and superstition with scientific thinking. For example, Pietro Albano (1250-1316) was condemned to death by the Inquisition for attempts to teach the known facts of medicine and what little was known of psychiatry. As the Renaissance was about to dawn, Arnold of Villanova (who was perhaps the most renowned physician of the Late Middle Ages and who also wrote a treatise on dream interpretation) was put to death for heresy because he tried to reconcile the principles of Hippocrates (the father of medicine) with the principles of demonology. Names almost forgotten now, such as Villanova, Maimonides, Roger Bacon, Raymond Lull, Peter Olivi, Pseudo-Galen, Peter of Spain, John of St. Almond, are but a few that appear on the rolls of those who sought a way out of their own darkness and tried to lead a reluctant mankind out of its intellectual night. It was—and still is—a lonely, pioneering era for those who seek the truth within the nature of both men's minds and their bodies.

Literature and art, too, reflect the same general flavor of thought. Dante's (1265-1321) *Divine Comedy*, perhaps the best-known literary work of that middle era of faith and superstition, gives a pretty accurate picture of this traditional view. The *Divine Comedy* is full of dreamlike symbology and expresses the human view of existence, heaven, hell, and purgatory—based on the accumulated religious and philosophical thought and superstition of a thousand years. The whole dream-poem itself symbolizes exactly where man, his mind and his spirit, had been and then stood in the twilight of the cruel, romantic, idealistic, chivalrous, hoping and groping middle era in the rise of Western Man as a being of intelligence and dignity. It begins with Dante's imagined descent into hell, guided by the ancient Roman poet, Virgil. It progresses downward to the depths, then upward, up the mountain of Purgatory, upward through the many concentric circles of heaven and enlightenment—from despair to hope of freedom until—

> The universe unfolds; all properties
> Of substance and of accident beheld,
> Compounded, yet one individual light
> The whole. And of such bonds methinks I saw
> The universe form; for where'er
> I do but speak of it, my soul dilates
> Beyond her proper self; and, till I speak,
> One moment seems a longer lethargy,
> Than five-and-twenty ages had appear'd
> To that emprise, the first made Neptune wonder
> At Argo's shadow darkening on his flood.
>
> Here vigor fail'd the Towering fantasy:
> But yet the will roll'd onward like a wheel
> In even motion by the love impell'd
> That moves the sun in heaven and all the stars.

Dante thus hopefully expressed the idea that man might ultimately see the totality and even infiniteness of his reality. Yet, ideas about the human psyche and the interpretation of its activity progressed little throughout the Renaissance, the Reformation and the early years of the Age of Reason. If anything, they became separated from scientific thinking, were largely left by the new breed of empiricists to the "make-believe" world of the religionist and the romantic or supernaturalist, and remain too much so today. Modern, rational man thus remains essentially out of touch with his inner self. He tends to think of the conscious level as all there is to him, when actually it is his lesser part. Because of our collective experience of the negative aspects of overemphasizing our other, psychic reality, we now reject it almost in its entirety. Somewhere, there is a happy medium, a point of view which allows for all aspects of reality—an educated, enlightened, eclectic approach.

GETTING BACK IN TOUCH

Perhaps the first modern thinker to begin to place thinking man back in touch with the reality and validity of other aspects of his being than the so-called rational and conscious was a man named Carl Gustav Carus (1789-1869). Carus postulated that the human psyche and its contents and activities did not necessarily belong in the world of fantasy or make-believe, but might also be valid subjects for scientific examination, intangible as they might seem. In a book entitled *Psyche*, he advanced the modern idea of the "unconscious" as the "key to understanding the essence of conscious processes." But he failed to devise any operational method of penetrating, examining and understanding the contents of this inner world. Such had to wait for the advent of Sigmund Freud. One of the main ways in which he opened the doorway into the human unconscious was in his empirical postulation that the dreams of human beings are real experiences representing valid data for scientific examination of the contents of the unconscious mind and being.

As most people know, Freud tended to overemphasize the sexual nature and aspects of the human psyche. One must remember, however, that he was a pioneer, an explorer of the inner space of the human mind. And few explorers can dictate the order in which they will discover the unknown. Had he lived longer, Freud undoubtedly would have discovered more. But his explorer's staff was taken up by others, the foremost of whom were Carl Gustav Jung and Alfred Adler, who looked further to find that there is more to the human psyche; that it actually is an infinitely and remarkably complex entity, made up of many parts, thoughts, functions, activities, responses and peculiarities—and that each human being is a distinct psychic individual as well as a part of society. Such thinkers came the farthest in developing the new psychology of self, particularly in seeing the role of dreams in relation to the human psyche, and in putting us back in touch with our whole selves. They developed the essential total perspective. There are very few sciences, studies or disciplines in which the maintaining of a total perspective is not of the utmost significance to obtaining as full an understanding as possible. Personality analysis (of oneself or someone else) is no exception. The greatest danger is to focus one's attention deep down into one aspect of that which is being considered at the expense of understanding the whole. To neglect to consider any part of the spectrum is tantamount to neglecting the whole self. Psychoanalysis (analysis of the human psyche) becomes particularly invalid when any atomistic approach is applied to it.

Jung also saw the necessity of the subjective point of view in psychoanalysis. He recognized that psychoanalysis is unlike other approaches in that external rules and collective dogma cannot be applied to it, that there are no norms or statistical measures, that every single analysis of every single person actually starts the process of psychoanalytical discovery all over again.

His basic hypothesis was that the unconscious does exist as a part of the human psyche, or personality, thereby confirming also the findings of others. But Jung went a step farther. He confirmed that the unconscious exists as an integral part of a total whole, which includes the conscious mind of man as well as his physiological being. He further confirmed that the unconscious itself consists of not one but several subelements of its own, which in turn are parts of both the whole unconscious and the whole person. He first published his "theory of personality" in a work called the *Psychology of the Unconscious* in 1917, which included the role of dreams.

Since then, more and more thoughtful and intelligent students and practitioners of psychoanalysis and psychotherapy have and continue to become convinced of the reality of both the unconscious and the significance of the dreams and other behavior that emerge from it. Today, a whole new psychology of self and "intouchness" has developed. Vast numbers of people once again are looking inwardly, to the inner person beneath the surface as perhaps the last hope of man on earth.

WHAT IS A DREAM?

You will have a more complete answer when you have read this whole book. Generally speaking, however, it may be said that a dream is a functional part of the self-adjustive mechanism that we call a human being. It is an occurrence within the inner world—the *unconscious* of a person. Dreaming is quite parallel to many of our physiological mechanisms. A dream is automatic and involuntary. Just as our physiological processes and mechanisms automatically try to rest when tired, or build antibodies to combat disease, or work to expel and reject impurities or foreign influences—so do our psyches function in a similar purposefully self-adjustive and self-defensive way. Recent research and experimentation substantiate this. In 1953 at the University of Chicago, several researchers conducted research on the dream activity of sleeping subjects under controlled laboratory conditions. These experiments had to do more with the observable physical activity of people while dreaming, and not the *content* of dreams, which is our main concern in this book. Freud and Jung still stand out as the major contributors to this latter research. But these experiments do relate to the reality of dreams and the fact that they are a functional part of the human mechanism.

As some readers may already know, these researchers made some interesting discoveries about sleep and dreaming. Using a complex instrument known as an *electroencephelograph*, which measures the electrical energy generated by the brain through electrodes attached to the scalp, they were able to objectively trace the rise and fall of the brain's activity during sleep. They identified distinct levels of sleep and isolated the level of brain activity at which most dreaming occurs. They also identified some other physical symptoms of dreaming. At regular intervals during sleep, the EEG showed an increase in brain activity. During these intervals, the eyes of sleeping subjects were observed to move rapidly beneath their eyelids. At the same time, there was an increased activity, such as twisting and jerking, observed in the extremities of the body, as if the brain were sending motor impulses to them. The researchers identified this period of sleep as the R.E.M. (rapid eye movement) period. This is when most dreaming occurs. When awakened abruptly during this period, sleepers consistently reported that they had been dreaming at the time.

Interestingly, these dreaming, or R.E.M., periods occurred at regular intervals during a night's sleep. That is, dreaming seemed to cycle. The sleepers dreamed, then seemed to fall off into a deeper level of sleep, seemed to rest or sleep within their sleep; dreamed again, rested again, etc., several times during a regular eight-hour sleeping period. It was almost as if, in this inner world of man, there was an additional cycle of "waking" and "sleeping," perhaps a lifetime in microcosm. In addition, something in the brain seemed to be treating this world as "real." For the brain sent definite impulses to the hands, the fingers, the feet, etc., to move and behave just as they do in waking. The body, in other words, was definitely trying to act out what the brain experienced.

The famous French scientist, Michel Jouvet, conducted another interesting experiment along the lines of this "acting out" phenomenon. It is known that animals, too, engage in some kind of "dream" activity. He actually was able to isolate the part of the brain in cats that is responsible for inhibiting full reaction of their bodies to the brain's impulses while dreaming. When he removed this portion of the cats' brains, the cats jumped up, and ran around the room hissing and mewing. But their eyes remained functionally closed, and they appeared oblivious to the environment around them. They remained, in fact, asleep, although they literally acted out their dreams. Whether or not experiments such as this will ever be conducted with humans remains to be seen.

The researchers then extended their experimentation to depriving people of their dreams to see what would happen. They repeatedly awakened subjects every time that it was found that they were dreaming. These people evidenced two distinct reactions. First, the more their dreaming was interrupted, the greater became the number of their R.E.M. periods; that is, the more did each seem to "try" to dream. Some self-adjustive mechanism in their makeups seemed to cause them to try to compensate for their loss of opportunities to "live" in this other world. Second, as these people continued to miss their dreaming, there was a definite effect upon their waking lives and personalities. Almost all became less adjusted in some way while awake. Some became more restless than before. Others became irritable. Some even evidenced neurotic behavior. And people totally deprived of sleep for extended periods began to hallucinate while awake. When normal sleep and dreaming were restored, and people were allowed their regular "quota" of life in the other world of sleep, they conversely settled down and became more normal in their waking lives. There is not yet a clear determination of how much misadjustment is the result of mere loss of sleep as opposed to loss of dreaming.

Such research does, however, substantiate the idea that dreaming definitely has *some* function in the maintenance of human equilibrium and stability. Dreams not only are real, they have a purpose and function as a part of the total human mechanism. In summary, it might be said that dreaming is the drama of life within the inner world of the human unconscious. More than this, it is a self-adjustive attempt of the human psychic mechanism to bring together, to more closely relate and integrate, our inner and outer realities into a balanced existence. In other words, a dream is an attempt to establish communication. It is an attempt of your inner being to bridge the gap between conscious and unconscious, seeking wholeness, unity and harmony, a very natural human instinct. A dream is a message. It is your unconscious mind's way of telling you things which it "thinks" you ought to know. As we shall see, the things that your unconscious might be telling you are as many and varied as are the possible contents of your dreams themselves.

SPECIFIC DREAMS HAVE SPECIFIC PURPOSES

Modern psychiatrists only recently have begun to do any extensive and intensive study into the *contents* of dreams as opposed to their physiological aspects, as in the experiments just described. We are now only beginning to swing wider the door to the human unconscious. One thing seems fairly certain so far: the *contents* of specific dreams seem to have highly individualistic purposes within the lives of the individual persons who have them. This may sound like an offhand statement. However, it actually represents an important basic approach of the psychoanalyst in finding a workable pathway into the vast inner workings of the mind of man. For once the purpose of a mechanism is discovered it is much easier to analyze the content that leads to that purpose.

THE LANGUAGE OF DREAMS

One of the reasons that we dismiss our dreams so readily is that we do not understand what they are saying. We do not understand what they are saying because they may speak in a language we are unaccustomed to in waking life. All language, of course, is symbolic. Words are not *the* things they describe; they merely represent those things. They are symbols. They are representations for ideas, feelings, and sensations that we experience. Suppose, for example, that you want to describe one of your feelings to another person. To do this, you can use words as symbols for what you think and feel. You undoubtedly often have experienced the inadequacy of words in conveying to another person exactly what it is that you are thinking and feeling. It would be infinitely better if you could somehow take the actual feeling, lift it out of yourself, and literally place it into the being of the other person so that he too could actually *experience* what you have experienced. This, in fact, would be the ultimate in interhuman communication. But, all to frequently, you must content yourself with using mere word symbols.

Simply stated, your inner self or unconscious is not burdened with the language barrier. For all of the experiences and feelings that it could want to convey to you are already stored within your mind. Since your unconscious is a part of your total mind, literally, all it has to do is call them forth and transmit them to your conscious mind. This is exactly what it does. And dreams are one of its primary mechanisms for doing so. The main difference is that your unconscious may or may not choose a symbol that your conscious mind immediately understands. Your conscious is conditioned to communicating verbally most of the time to begin with. The unconscious usually uses nonverbal symbols. Thus, there is a basic switching over from a verbal to a nonverbal orientation. For example, suppose that your unconscious wishes to communicate to you the idea "table." This is exactly what a table really is to your mind—an *idea*, even more, perhaps a *feeling*, or even better an *experience*. There are many kinds and sizes and shapes of "table-experiences." The single word table will rarely be sufficient to convey the full table-experience. The unconscious, however, already has an *exact* image of exactly *the* table it wants to show you. It needs merely to retrieve that image and let you "see" it. And this is what it will do.

Take this reasoning a step farther. A table-experience, despite its possible variations, is a relatively simple thing to portray. But what about an anxiety-experience, a hope-experience, or some other emotion-laden experience? Or, for that matter, what about the experience of roundness, instead of merely a table? Or what about the sense of wholeness that is experienced in roundness? What about an emotional need, or fear? All of these things, along with the tables, the automobiles, the people, the houses, etc., that you experience are also stored in you unconscious.

Basically what your unconscious does, when it is impelled to communicate with your conscious, is to select from its vast store of experiences any image or action that will convey what it is trying to express. Suppose, for example, that your deep-seated self is seeking wholeness, and unity and homogeneity, those feelings and ideas that are quite well-expressed in terms of roundness, or a circle, perhaps a circular table. Suppose further that this deep-seated need for wholeness is very similar to some feelings that you experienced as a child. Basically, what your unconscious is quite likely to do is to select a table as a part of its dream-message. But it will not select just *any* table from the many that it has seen and recorded. It will select *the* one that most closely symbolizes the whole thing it is trying to say. Or, if a group of people (perhaps some long-dead) is more appropriate, this is what you will dream of, perhaps a circular gathering of people.

Your conscious mind, so accustomed to the verbal language symbology, in addition to having long since stored away some of the original impressions represented in the dream symbols, is quite likely to miss the true significance of, say, the simple appearance of the old family dining room table in a dream that may have several other equally obscure experience-symbols in it. Not the least among the confusing factors, also, is that your unconscious is not bound by the restrictions of logical sequence, time, and space that bind your conscious thinking. It is just as likely to choose a twenty-year-old symbol as a day-old one. For example, last night one of the authors dreamed of a World War II Japanese colonel. This is why long-dead or forgotten people often appear in the present reality of your dreams, as if they are still alive. In fact, as far as the unconscious is concerned, they are still alive.

This is the basic nature of the language in which dreams speak. It also is part of the reason that many dreams are not readily understood, and are consequently dismissed as meaningless. When you understand how the unconscious expresses itself you gain a new insight into *all* of your behavior, both waking and sleeping. We shall see much more about the symbolic language of the unconscious, and by the time you finish reading this book, you should be at least sufficiently knowledgeable to "listen" to that language in a more informed way. For the moment, it is enough to call your attention to the fact that the unconscious speaks in a unique symbolic language, and that without an understanding of that language it will be next to impossible for you to understand what yours is telling you.

EVERYONE DREAMS

We should clear up another matter here in passing. You may have heard some people say that they do not dream. So far as can be determined, everyone dreams. Some of us simply do not remember our dreams, and there are significant reasons that we do not. Remember that the human mechanism is self-adjustive. One of the main reasons that we do not remember is that, like many other mechanisms within us, dreaming operates automatically. That is, if a given dream accomplishes its purpose as a part of our internal programming, it is duly noted within us, and life goes on normally without undue fanfare. Just as, for example, when we cry or laugh we release pent-up emotions and then feel better, one of the functions of dreaming is to act as a kind of automatic "safety valve." In the uninhibited self-world of sleep, the dream permits us to relieve pressures or anxieties that are difficult to work off in the waking world.

The second main reason that we do not remember some dreams is more significant. In psychological terms, we may be *repressing* them. We may be hiding from ourselves. This can be dangerous and represents one of the best reasons for trying to remember and to interpret them. The more we hide from our inner selves, the more open do we become to invasion from our inner worlds. Needless to say, if one represses too much for too long, internal pressures continue to build up. A point of breakdown may be reached.

Sometimes, the barriers in the mind are not strong enough to prevent particularly traumatic inner experiences from breaking through into our waking minds. This is how we remember some dreams that we really don't want to know about. We also will remember a dream when it does not constitute a threat to anything in our consciousness. There is also, of course, the matter of *ignoring* one's dreams. There is not very much that anyone other than the dreamer himself can do about this. Obviously, we do not recommend this as a desirable course of action.

In any case, *everyone* dreams, and their dreams have valid and meaningful things to tell them—if they have ears to hear. They not only can relieve tension and tell you how well-adjusted you are to life's vagaries and vicissitudes, but can often warn you of things that are threatening that adjustment. They often will tell you what you should do to *avert* an oncoming breakdown or dysfunction in the delicate balance that keeps your whole conscious and unconscious mechanism stable.

With a little effort of will and discipline, you soon will be able to remember what goes on in your inner world of sleep and begin to accumulate a working body of valuable information about yourself, hitherto unknown to you. One of the best ways to accumulate the information base is to keep a written daily record of your dreams. For, as you know, most of their contents will otherwise escape you. A later chapter contains some suggestions on how to keep a dream diary.

DREAM INTERPRETATION IS HIGHLY PERSONAL

There is another important factor that frequently gives people trouble in realistically approaching their own dreams. This is that dream interpretation is very *individualistic*. This is highly important. *All* valid psychoanalysis and psychotherapy, of which dream interpretation is a branch, are *personal*. There is no external test or norm that can be applied to determine how "valid" or "right" an interpretation is. The external norm or statistical approach of the behavioral psychologist has no bearing in dream interpretation. How things are with *other people* really has very little bearing in any form of self-adjustment. Many psychologists seem to think that if someone conforms to or does what a certain percentage of the population does, he is "normal" or "adjusted." This is quite ridiculous when you stop to think about it. How can what anyone else has done possibly be a measure of how well-adjusted you are *inside you*? Fortunately, these dehumanized statistical approaches are rapidly being discarded among intelligent and informed evaluators of human behavior. Our point is that you will never be able to "look up" the interpretation of your dream in some textbook or catalog. The meaning of a dream is never found in a theory of interpretation, but in the dream itself. The purpose and interpretation of your dream may be similar to someone else's dreams, but this can be determined only *after* you have found out what *your* dream means to you. You will find that we have included a list of common dream symbols in this book. But we have done so for a different purpose, which will be explained later.

It may help to remember that even when you go to a professional analyst, his so-called "objective" analysis of you can, and often does, become nothing more than another externally imposed test or set of criteria. If both of you are not very careful, it can be an analysis of what *he* thinks and feels and experiences, not what *you* think and feel and experience. The analysis could be as much an analysis of him as of you; at best, an analysis of your relationship. One must remember that even the "scientists" themselves are subjective personalities, and can never divest themselves of their own selves. Psychoanalysis can never be depersonalized or objectivized in the way that parts of, say, chemistry or physics or mathematics might. In evaluating the human psyche, everything must be considered from the inner, subjective point of view—which itself is a part of the data. This is why it is so important for the psychoanalyst to find out as much as he possibly can about what his subject is thinking, feeling, sensing, and experiencing, both rationally and irrationally. This is the only sound data base for analysis; not some behavioral curve or chart.

Dream interpretation is thus very subjective. The data with which you work is exclusively *your* material. The statistical "rules" of how *other* people act and react are not relevant, merely of interest. The serious interpreter of dreams, therefore, must take what may be a new view of the subjective approach—if he is a typical modern thinker. For most of us have been conditioned to reject subjectivity. We are suspicious of any phenomenon that cannot be explained objectively according to some external criteria. Subjectivity presumably has no place in the thinking of the "intelligent, well-adjusted person." Science downgrades the subjective experience as a danger to sound thinking. Our mores and religions tell us that it is wrong to be selfish and ego-centered. Yet, everything that goes on inside of each of us remains a totally subjective experience. Society must, of course, protect itself from the unbridled or dangerously arrant self-experience. But, when it comes to an individual person's evaluation of himself and his adjustment to his own inner and outer worlds, the *only* thing that matters is *his* subjective experiencing of these worlds. We, of course, speak of such adjustment on a broad and balanced level, which includes an adjustment to the society and environment in which we live.

The key, then, is to accept and allow for the fact that the subjective view is totally valid in dream interpretation. Your dreams are exclusively *your* data. Their contents, logical or illogical, rational or irrational, can be evaluated only in terms of themselves and the self-whole of which they are a part.

THE APPROACH CAN BE SCIENTIFIC

The empirical, scientific approach, however, can and should be applied. You are dealing with a body of information, a data base—your subjective experience. To derive meaning, relationship, or correlation, you must still examine that data piece by piece. In other words, what you really must do is approach your subjectivity objectively. You must, as it were, view all happenings from both inside and outside yourself.

What you will be doing in analyzing your dreams, if your approach is sound, is proceeding exactly as any scientist proceeds in gathering evidence and formulating and testing a hypothesis. The purpose and meaning *will always emerge from the data*. Never can an external purpose be assigned, and the data then selected to support it.

Fortunately, the contents of your dreams are not the only data you have to work with in determining the purposes and meanings of your dreams. A sound approach demands also that you understand the nature of the environment in which your dreams occur. They occur totally within your psyche. Your psyche *is* the environment. To proceed without an understanding of what your psyche is and how it functions would be operating in a vacuum. It has also been quite well-substantiated, as already mentioned, that dreams "speak" in a unique language, a symbolic language. And to proceed without understanding that language would be like trying to understand someone speaking in a language you have never heard.

Of no small importance, also, is the work that others have done in the field of dream interpretation—the empirical discoveries that already have been made. A simple example will give insight into the importance of the total perspective and the empirical approach, as well as the nature of the language of dreams, and the value of knowing what others have discovered. Take, for example, the common dream of flying or levitation which almost everyone has had at one time or another in his or her life. In fact, dream analysts undoubtedly have recorded thousands, perhaps millions, of such dreams by their clients and patients. Human beings, of course, do not actually fly, and it is quite unlikely that any sane, awake person would try. Yet, in the sleeping world, all things can be experienced. A part of the dreamer's mind wants the experience of flying and therefore has it. The next question is, why would anyone want to fly? There are many possible answers. He might want to get *above* things, perhaps the multitude of trivia and frustrations that confront him as he walks about on the ground. Height traditionally symbolizes strength and power. Flying is a transcending, releasing experience. It also is a form of escape. Many pilots actually refer to it as the last place on earth where a man can be free and unrestricted. "Going higher" also frequently bespeaks a striving toward some goal or wish, perhaps the dream of grandeur and accomplishment so common to youth and unrealistically immature adults. Flying is used in waking life as a symbol for many things. We thus already begin with a certain universal symbolic meaning. The dream thus already stands a very good chance of being a *symbol* for something other than the actual act of moving through the air, just as flying often is metaphoric in waking life. Add to this what it might mean to you personally, and you come up with what is probably a pretty good interpretation of what your particular dream of flying might mean. Dreams of flying, incidentally, are much more common among younger people.

The total perspective is still important. The *circumstances* under which one is flying in his dream are extremely significant, for example, whether or not one is flying in an airplane, what he is flying over, where or what he is flying to, etc. Also of importance is the *total life experience* of the dreamer and his *current psychic situation*. These last two also are a highly significant part of the empirical data base and must be integrated into the interpretation. In fact, there is a maxim in dream interpretation: "always start with your current conscious situation."

The point here, however, is that enough analysts have examined enough flying dreams, and empirically seen enough commonness and similarity in *all* flying dreams to be able to at least tentatively derive an hypothesis that there is a reasonable chance that the next dream of flying that they examine will have a purpose and meaning similar to all of the others they have examined. But our basic warning still applies here. *Your* dream is solely and exclusively *your* material. The experiences of others may or may not serve as a measurement for your experience. However, they most certainly could serve as an *aid* to you in determining what such a dream is *likely* to mean. There are many other common dream experiences—dreams of falling, dying, nakedness, losing teeth, killing, sex, unknown presences, drowning, choking, and many others—from which it is possible to derive the same sort of generalized function and meaning. Yet, to go to a catalog or listing to look up the meaning of your dream is the wrong approach. Flying, for example, could mean that one has an inflated opinion of one's self, doesn't have his "feet on the ground," etc. But it could also be that one is merely the kind of person who would like to become a pilot. The best approach, therefore, remains the empirical one. You will start off on the right track if you retain a total perspective and consider *all* of the data and factors just mentioned— your dream content, your total life situation, your current life situation, and *then* what this or that catalog says your dream *might* mean, which might merely be suggestive in starting a chain of associations to find the application to you.

WHO SHOULD INTERPRET DREAMS

Most people are at least partially aware that dreams

represent things that occur in the deeper recesses of their own minds. There is a relatively widespread belief that only a "trained" psychologist should explore those deeper recesses. The simple truth is that *you* have as much right to understand and interpret your own inner world as anyone else has. In fact, this is precisely what any psychiatrist or psychoanalyst encourages you to do. For he knows that the solutions to your mental and emotional problems can come from only one place—inside you. We shall quickly point out, however, that we in no way downgrade the seeking of trained, professional help in cases where the dysfunction of your inner mechanisms has reached a point where you can no longer cope with them. It is our premise here, however, that, in cases where severe neurosis is not involved, individual persons have every right to and ought to interpret their own dreams.

The main reason that people do not look more deeply into their personal dream activity is fear. Even when a person says he doesn't care about what his dreams may be telling him, he probably is covering up the fact that he is afraid to know his inner self. He may be afraid that he is not as well-adjusted as he tells himself and the world that he is. He may see danger in knowing too much about himself, or mistakenly think that if he ignores warning signs, they may go away. However, it is more dangerous *not* to know what our dreams are saying.

Many of us tend to forget just how shortly removed we are from the superstitious thinking of an earlier era. The flame of enlightenment burns slowly. The legacy of darkness, superstition and misinterpretation of the psychic world left to us by our forebears has yet to be dispensed with in its entirety. As we have seen, the modern psychological view of man's mind and psyche did not even begin to obtain a foothold until the nineteenth century. As late as the eighteenth century, men were still put to death for "conjuring" and witchcraft. Thus, there remains within all of us an association of dreams with the mysterious, the occult, and the "unreal." Many of us are still afraid of the dark and still expect some spirit or ghost to emerge from the night. We prefer to pull the covers up over our heads and to hide from whatever is out there in the dark that threatens us. The fact is that there *is* a psychic world as real as the physical world, or we would feel no threat. The threat itself is psychic, and real, founded or unfounded as it might be. But instead of confronting the threat and its nature, and asking the voices in the night to what purpose they are "speaking" to us, we pretend that they are not there. If we were truly the scientific, rational people that we claim we are, we would address these inner- or other-worldly voices and derive evidence from them. In any case, unfounded superstitions must be dispensed with if one is to understand the real nature and meaning of his dream life.

We realize that these things may take a little personal courage for some, and for others a great deal of courage. For it is true that there often is no more fearsome world than the one which one finds within his own being. But this is also the world from which the only true victory in life can come. The payoff is well worth the effort in terms of the valuable information and insights one obtains. For they indeed represent an opening to the boundless possibilities of self-discovery and its ensuing victorious individual life. There is no more appropriate way to describe the interpretation of your dreams than as a *doorway to your unconscious*, perhaps even to your soul itself.

SUMMARY

Dreams, therefore, are definitely real. There also can be no doubt that they have definite purposes in your total

makeup as a human being. As to the specific purposes and
interpretations of specific dreams, yours or anyone else's,
these remain to be determined as you gain a knowledge of
the psychic "territory" in which you are operating and an
understanding of the language in which dreams speak. You
should, by now, be moving steadily toward an insight into
how your inner world of self functions and a firm base for
understanding the language that is its currency. If, at this
point, you are willing to acknowledge your own unconscious in the way just described, it is now time to take a
closer look at the *figures* in your unconscious—the forms in
which you inner mind structures its contents, especially in
your dreams.

Before doing this, however, it might be well for you to
stop for a moment or two and try to actually take a first
confronting and acknowledging look at your own unconscious. There is nothing terribly esoteric or difficult about
doing this. It is primarily a matter of emptying your mind
of interfering thoughts, being receptive, and concentrating.
Read the following instructions.

1. Set aside a period of time immediately before you
   plan to retire tonight as a special meditative period.
2. Spend this time in a relaxed and quiet setting,
   perhaps propped up in bed ready to go to sleep.
3. Do not read anything. If possible, it will help to
   have a favorite painting where you can observe it.
   Or, you can merely paint your own picture of your
   favorite setting in your mind. Almost any picture,
   real or imagined, will serve the purpose.
4. Begin by simply concentrating on the scene and
   trying to empty your mind of all thoughts except
   your observation.
5. As you relax, study the details of the image in your
   mind. Gradually, try to project yourself into the
   scene. Imagine that you are actually in the picture.

6. As you continue to relax, turn off the light and settle down in your favorite sleeping position. Gradually, transfer your mental focus from the scene you have been "watching" and participating in, backward into yourself.

7. Become aware of how it feels inside your body and mind. Now consciously acknowledge the existence of your inner self—your unconscious. Say to yourself that you acknowledge this inner you. But do not merely verbalize, *realize and attempt to experience* this inner self; *accept* it as a fact, just as you would accept the existence of any other fact. *Know it*.

8. Now, "open" yourself; concentrate on *feeling* open and receptive toward what is inside of you.

9. *Decide* that tonight, as you dream, you are going to observe what is going on with a new awareness, a new acceptance. Look expectantly into the night, into yourself.

10. Continue feeling this way until you drop off to sleep.

11. In the morning, as soon as you awaken, take paper and record every detail that you have dreamed. Record the following.*

   — The persons in your dream with as accurate a description of each as you can recall.

   — The location and setting of the dream.

   — The action or narrative that took place.

   — The feelings you have about this dream; for example, fear, horror, peacefulness, happiness, melancholy, etc.

If you have not dreamed, do not worry. Actually, as we have explained, you probably did dream. You merely do

---

*Detailed instruction for keeping a dream diary is given in Chapter 11.

not remember it. In any case, each evening, upon retiring, "get ready to dream." Start whenever possible with a meditative period before hand. If you cannot always do this, begin when you get into bed.

If you are faithful in the motivation and practice just described, or even merely in developing a sense of personal desire and openness toward encountering your inner world of self, you will find the doorway swinging ever wider. It has been said that there is nothing that will not give up its secrets if it is loved enough. This could not be truer of anything than it is of one's own self.

5

The Unknown Presence

With a basic understanding of the structure of the unconscious (remembering that "structure" is at best a loosely fitting term), it is possible to look more closely at some of the contents of the unconscious, and particularly how some of them manifest themselves in our dreams. The dream itself, of course, occurs totally within the self. It is important to remain aware of just how *personal* and *subjective* is your inner, unconscious realm. It is a realm vastly different from the outer world that you experience in waking and consciousness. It is the world of self. In the outer world, there are many points of reference. One can observe, as a bystander, all sorts of facts, occurrences and phenomena, and see how they relate to one another as well as to self. When one navigates—his person, a ship, an airplane, or even a spacecraft—in the outer world, there is always *some* farther point, perhaps a landmark or a star, to which to refer in order to determine one's position and relationship. Imagine, however, navigating in or observing a total void—the only point of reference being the spot where you stand at any given moment. In your unconscious, there *is* nothing external or objective against which to measure any fact or event other than how it relates to self. Self is the point of reference, the "center of the universe."

In a dream, the self expands beyond what it appears to be at a given moment of consciousness. While you are awake, only one main aspect of your personality is present at any given moment. This is not true within your unconscious. *All aspects of your personality are simultaneously present.* In a very real way, that oft-repeated conscious wish that "I could be several people at the same time" comes true. Your many selves are both present and active.

This should not be too difficult to conceive if you stop and think of how it *has* to be inside you mind. All of the things have to be there at once, coexistent. There is nowhere else that they could be. There is no sequence. In the conscious world, there is sequence. The time factor is present. Something happens in the present, immediately becomes the past, and another approaching event succeeds, takes the place of, that which just happened. In the unconscious, there is only one tense: the present. There is neither a logical nor a time sequence. At best, there is merely a competition, as it were, among the contents as to which of them will come before the attention of the viewer (which is you) at any given moment.

With this in mind, it is easy to see why conditions change so rapidly in a dream. For example, at one moment the dreamer may be in one location and suddenly, in a split second, find himself in another, miles and eons of time away from the first. Or, two events, which could never do so in reality, can even occur simultaneously. The dreamer may even become a totally different person, perhaps a young child again. The past child that he once was is also stored in the present memory of his unconscious—perhaps on a "shelf" right alongside the adult that he was five, two, or a year ago . . . or yesterday. It may be difficult to conceive, but there simply are no categories of time, space or logical sequence in the unconscious. Anything that has sufficient strength at the moment can and does come into the field of "vision."

When one sees the true subjective nature of his own inner world of unconsciousness and the simultaneous nature of its contents, it should not be too difficult to see how dreams really function. Couple this knowledge with the known fact that there actually are many personalities totally within the self, to whom could these personalities perform their roles, manifest their characteristics, assert their needs, tell their problems? There is no one other than the self of which they are a part. You become at once author, actor and audience in the life-drama that takes place within your own mind.

Dreams, the inner life-drama, contain all the elements that the waking, outer life-drama contains—people, settings or environment, and events or action. When we say that dreams are *symbolic*, we do not mean that they are symbolic from the inner point of view. They are actual and real there. We mean that they are symbolic from the *interpretive* point of view because they do not speak in verbal language. The unconscious has no need of language to represent or describe an event, setting, person, or representation of part of the dreamer's personality. It already has the original experience or image that the language would describe. For example, it does not have to describe to you the child part of your personality because the child itself is in you—in your mind. It actually can be you and be experienced and seen by you. The same goes for objects and feelings and attitudes.

If you will analyze for a moment how it really is in your conscious life, you also will see a little more clearly how it is in your inner, unconscious life. In waking life, you walk around, do things, interact with your environment and other people, etc. If there were no "you," there would be none of these. In other words, you are the observer and interpreter of your conscious life experience. This is why Descartes said, "I think, therefore I am." He merely confirmed the obvious—that self is the center of the universe, and that the experiencing and observing of life *is* your life. In waking life, there is only one "you"—your conscious self—doing the living and experiencing. (In reality, all of your selves exert an influence, but we are not arguing this point here. For the purpose of the moment it is sufficient merely to describe your conscious self in the singular.) In a dream, there is this fundamental difference: Not only is your conscious self active and doing the living, but all your many selves are. And each is in fact a self. Each is a "you," in addition to the conscious "you" also present.

This does not mean that the conscious "you" necessarily has any greater capability to recognize the full nature of your other selves than it does in waking life. Nevertheless, these other selves are "walking beside" or living with the conscious you. Often, however, you may be only vaguely aware of their presence. You frequently cannot see their faces in a dream. What you usually are aware of, more than any actual face, is a certain *kind* of person, a kind of *shadow figure*, not fully defined or identified. The shadow figure in your dream is a representation of some facet of your personality, partially or fully hidden or repressed from your conscious awareness, but still living and functioning.

One might realize the full meaning of this by recalling the popularized real-life story of a few years ago entitled *The Three Faces of Eve*. Here was a case in which a person's shadow figures actually broke through the barrier that normally exists between the conscious and the unconscious worlds. For some unique set of reasons within this particular person (not yet fully understood), her shadow figures, or other personalities, did not remain either in her dreams or confine themselves to the deeper recesses of her mind while she was awake. They actually took over the functions of her physical body and were able to overrule her conscious restraint of them. Psychiatrists were able to observe what for all intents and purposes was a dream in action in a conscious person. They saw three distinct people in the same person. At one moment, this woman would be her "normal" self—that is, the external person that she and the rest of the world knew as "her." At another moment, a completely different personality would take over her person. Far from the relatively plain person that the woman ordinarily was, this other person was a dark, even evil, being. She was promiscuous, selfish, often vile in language and behavior. Suddenly, at times, for no apparent reason, another totally different person would appear. Facial expression, stance, tastes, language— everything—would change. The observer would see standing before him a marvelously poised and sophisticated female, speaking and behaving in an ideal and attractive way. Then, without warning, the "original woman" would reappear, who was demure, unsure of herself, even "mousy." Among many interesting aspects of this phenomenon was the fact that these three personalities, all existing in the same person, *knew of each other* and actually competed for possession of the woman's conscious faculties. In each case, the woman actually became *the* person, one of her shadow selves. Her doctors were even able to converse with each "person" as a separate being.

One cannot help thinking of the New Testament story of Jesus casting out the "demons."

> And when he was come out of the ship, immediately there met him out of the tombs a man with an unclean spirit,
>
> Who had *his* dwelling among the tombs; and no man could bind him, no, not with chains:
>
> Because that he had been often bound with fetters and chains, and the chains had been plucked asunder by him, and the fetters broken in pieces, neither could any *man* tame him.
>
> And always, night and day, he was in the mountains, and in the tombs, crying, and cutting himself with stones.
>
> But when he saw Jesus afar off, he ran and worshipped him.
>
> And cried with a loud voice, and said, What have I to do with thee, Jesus, *thou* Son of the most high God? I adjure thee by God, that thou torment me not.
>
> For he said unto him, Come out of the man, *thou* unclean spirit.
>
> And he asked him, what *is* thy name? And he answered, saying, My name *is* Legion: for we are many.

Who or what were this man's "demons"? Perhaps, and quite likely, they were his many selves. Once addressed and confronted for what they really were by the "great physician," they "came out of him." And once Eve and her psychiatrists addressed and confronted her other two selves, gave them their just due and assurances of expression, they too "came out of her," or, perhaps more accurately, were integrated back into her where they belonged.

The classic literary example of this multiple personality phenomenon, of course, is *Dr. Jekyl and Mr. Hyde.* But Eve was an actual case and conclusive proof of the "many selves" concept. The significant fact is that neither she, nor Dr. Jekyl, nor "Legion," were alone. The only real difference was that their other selves had penetrated more into the conscious realm. In most of us, these varying selves merely take momentary control. A mature, middle-aged man, for example, temporarily behaves like a pouting child. Or, on the other hand (for all of our selves are not negative), a normally frustrated, nervous, fearful housewife momentarily takes command of a situation and becomes a mature, fully coping, decisive adult, capable of sound judgment, decision and action.

Some modern psychological writers have hypothesized that within each of us there are at least three distinct divisions of personality or actual personalities: a child, a parent, and an adult. In actuality, there are more likely many instead of merely three sides of our personalities. At various times and representing a variety of personal relationships to self and to external life, say these writers, each of these persons has his or her "say so" in our conscious behavior. When a person begins to observe and accept himself or herself as not one but many selves, this is when he or she begins to productively understand his or her true self and to work upon and improve that self.

Recognition, bringing out into the light of day the various positive and negative aspects of our personalities, our demons and our better selves, calling them by their name—perhaps "Legion" is as good a name as any for all of us—this is one of the main keys to inner light.

We should also reemphasize here that all our "shadows" are not negative or destructive. Many of the hidden aspects of our psyches have a high contributory and productive value. Even some of the so-called negative aspects, such as the child within each of us, have a legitimate right to expression in our lives. There is nothing inherently wrong, for example, in behaving capriciously or selfishly on occasion. The key is *balance and harmony*. Remember, you do not have to apologize for being a human being. This balance and harmony, however, can never be attained so long as you look at yourself, and when you say "I," think that you are but one. If you are *really* seeking self-knowledge and self-mastery, you must, as Machiavelli observed, "deal with things as they really are—not as we might wish them to be."

WHAT TO DO WITH YOUR SHADOWS

The answer is simple but requires considerable effort of will and discipline to put into action. You must *confront* and *embrace* your shadows. You must even *befriend* and *love* them. You must see who and what they are within you. You must fulfill their needs just as you fulfill the needs of your conscious self. You must assuage their fears and anxieties, reassure and comfort them. In so doing, you will be ministering to yourself, for they are you—the total you. In so befriending your shadows, your many selves, you will begin to live in harmony and at peace within yourself. A series of dreams recently reported to us by a young woman points up some of these things.

Joanne is a thirty-year-old housewife married for nine years to a successful young stockbroker. She and Jim have two lovely daughters aged four and two, and an eight-year-old son. Externally, Joanne seemed quite adjusted, gregarious and happy with her present status as a wife and mother living in an affluent suburb. But this was only what the outside observer saw. Internally, Joanne was suffering from what we have come to call the "trapped-suburban-housewife syndrome," because we have seen it so often.

Joanne met Jim in college. He was majoring in economics; she, fashionably, in psychology. They both graduated the same year, and within a month were married. The story from there on is almost classic in our present society. The first child was born within the year. They both agreed that she should not be a "working mother" for all the standard reasons. For all the standard reasons also, Jim began his struggle to climb the ladder in his career and also to provide his new family with all the accoutrements of affluence. Over the nine years of their marriage, he had taken night courses to improve his basic business skill, often worked part-time jobs for extra money, and frequently worked extra in his regular job. The net result was that Joanne spent much time alone in the isolation of their "lovely" suburban home which, of course, they could not have afforded if Jim just worked his eight-to-five job. Just as the first child reached school age, the second came along, renewing Joanne's restrictions. No sooner was she out of diapers than the third child arrived. Somehow, too, the reasons for Jim's long absences from home continued. Often, night after night, Joanne would find herself with little more company than a television set, a sinkful of dishes, a full laundry hamper and a toy-strewn living room floor. But she yearned for more. This history could continue in more detail, but you have merely to look across the street, down the hall to the next apartment, or perhaps into your own home to find the rest of the story.

Nevertheless, when we first became acquainted with Joanne, what we saw beneath the well-groomed, externally polished and articulate facade of the wife of a successful stockbroker, was our familiar "trapped suburban housewife." She could not hide the tightness of her lips and chin, the traces of stridency and tautness in her vocal cords, the underlying irritability and exasperation. After years of professionally observing people, we are rarely fooled by their external appearance or terribly surprised by most of the contents of their dreams. So it was with Joanne's. The first dream she reported to us follows:

> I was in a very large and well-furnished mansion. There were many statues and works of art among the furnishings. There was someone with me, taller than me and, I think, more mature and sophisticated. She had a very calm and decisive voice. I know I was frightened by her, too. Then, I saw at the top of a stairway a little girl in a party dress. She started down the stairs, with what I think was a doll in her arms. I suddenly was aware that the person with me had a butcher knife from my kitchen in her hand. The child saw the knife at the same time I did. The evil nature of this woman beside me suddenly became fully apparent to me. She started toward the child, and I knew she was going to kill it. The child started to run back up the stairs, and this other person started after her. I could not move. I screamed, or called out something; I don't know what. The person stopped and turned. The face wasn't clear, but in a way it was clear. The eyes glared at me and there was a wicked smile. The person started back toward me. I remember thinking, "I've at least saved the child." But now the person was after me. I started to run away, through the many rooms of the big house, trying to find a way out. But every door I opened just led to another room. This went on, I don't know how long. Then suddenly I had nowhere else to run. She approached me, raised the knife, grinning evilly, and plunged it downward. I screamed some unintelligible words and woke up in a fright.

As usually is the case, the mere fact of knowing something about the larger life-situation of the person sheds considerable light on this dream. The setting of the dream, of course, has significance. But we are primarily interested in the characters at this time. We selected this particular dream because it is a more or less classic "shadow dream" and clearly shows how a person's shadow selves can appear simultaneously in multiple form, and how the dreamer's conscious can function as observer *and* player in the dream-drama.

Who, first, is the little girl in the dream? It could be one of Joanne's children. But this is unlikely. For, in all probability, the child would appear as herself. This child is a "stranger." It is far more likely that it is the child-part of Joanne. It is the part of Joanne that still is the happy, contented, secure child that she was in her earlier life. We have some indication of this from the dress of the child and, as Joanne further described, her appearing clean, groomed and dressed for a happy occasion. The child seemed to reveal no particular frightened or traumatic aspect, and just disappeared from view when threatened. But she was threatened. Something or someone within Joanne wanted to do away with this immature but happy figure. Little girls, of course, play—they play house, they play mother, as this child apparently was doing with the doll in her arms. Could there be a part of Joanne that is merely "playing" at being a grown-up mother, a part that doesn't want to accept the reality that she is in fact a grown-up, responsible woman?

Second, who is this known but unknown presence as Joanne described her? She seems mature. She is taller than Joanne, or at least seems to be. Perhaps she stands more erectly and decisively. Now, why does she want to kill this child part? What is killing? It is eliminating something, is it not? But the child disappears. What else in the setting might need eliminating? Could it be that part or all of the conscious person that Joanne is needs eliminating? Can this other person standing beside the observer—this other self—be more aware, more able to compare what Joanne is with what she was or could be or wants to be?

Recall the dream of the young man walking along the cliff. The person trying to destroy him also was a shadow self—a partial personality—a destructive part of his personality. In the above case, the shadow, although it seems bent on killing, may not actually be totally destructive. For, the elimination of part of Joanne's conscious existence actually would be beneficial. There thus is a subtle difference between the shadow of the young man and Joanne's shadow.

We continued to counsel with Joanne and to have her report her dreams to us. Invariably this "other" woman was present in some form. In most of the dreams, she appeared almost the same. She became revealed over the course of time as a not altogether negative personage. Often, she appeared in partially comforting, leader-type relationships to Joanne. Joanne actually liked her and felt relatively secure with her presence in the dream. Yet, she frequently tried to do away with Joanne as the conscious observer.

We gradually approached with Joanne the possibility of her not running away when the figure tried to kill her. We also knew, however, that so long as corrective action was not taken in Joanne's real conscious life, the whole situation and its interpretation would remain theoretical. At our urging, Joanne, with her degree in psychology, was able to obtain part-time work in a psychiatrist's office as a general assistant. Here she became exposed to numerous upset and dysfunctioning persons. Over the better part of a year, she gradually developed a sympathetic, definitely more mature demeanor toward the people her employer was trying to help. She developed a new conscious role in life. In speaking with her employer, we found that he saw her as a well-adjusted, very helpful and dependable person of gentle and understanding personality. He mentioned to us that she was precisely the type of person he wanted in his front office.

Finally, after almost two years, the 'phone call we had been expecting and hoping for came. Excitedly and hurriedly, because she was on the way to her new-found fulfillment in life, Joanne called us one morning and quickly related the following dream. This is exactly the way she put it:

> I confronted my shadow last night. I saw this woman. We were in a wide field. She came toward me with some weapon or instrument in her hand. I was still scared. But as I started to turn and run, for some reason, something made me stop. I was very frightened. But I stood there as she came toward me to strike me Then I did something. I smiled at her and I actually stretched my arms out as if to embrace her. I stood there. quaking in my shoes. But, would you believe that she stopped dead in her tracks. She cocked her head to one side and looked at me very curiously. Then, she actually smiled, and she turned and walked away, very erect, away across that big field. Do you believe that?

The wide open field, as opposed to the house described in the earlier dream also had some fairly obvious significance. But the real significance was that Joanne had confronted and dealt with a part of her self. And although we know that she has other shadows, and may dream other frightening dreams in her lifetime, she has learned to live in harmony with at least one of her many selves.

HOW TO IDENTIFY YOUR SHADOWS

As we have said, the average person usually has many different shadow figures within his unconscious; that is, many partial or, as Jung called them, splinter personalities which from time-to-time attempt to manifest themselves. Your whole objective is, of course, to be able to identify, understand and deal with these parts of your personality in an intelligent and useful way. The first step, therefore, is to be able to recognize them when you see them in a dream. There are several important things that you can do that will help you in this effort:

1. *Be Ready:* Begin right now to develop in yourself an attitude of readiness and willingness to meet these figures in your dreams. Look forward, even with anticipation, to the encounters that you will have as you dream. Decide and repeat to yourself in

your conscious mind that you are open and accepting toward these other parts of your personality. Each night, as you fall asleep, practice this feeling of acceptance and willingness to see and embrace these "people" as they will inevitably appear in your dreams.

2. *Be Observant:* It may seem unlikely to think that you can, in your conscious mind, make decisions that will carry over and apply to what happens in your sleep. This is because you are accustomed to the involuntary nature of what happens in your dreams. You are accustomed to standing helplessly by and letting things happen. The truth is, however, that you actually can exercise some control in the dream-drama that your conscious observes and participates in. After all, it still is your conscious mind, with the same decision-making capability that it has in the waking state. What it really amounts to more than anything else is a matter of training, convincing, and conditioning yourself to carry that decision-making ability over into the dream world.

This is not necessarily easy, but it can be done, and it is the main key to your beginning to control what is going on inside yourself instead of being controlled by those conditions and events. You are capable of more than you may think. If you continue and persist in your determination to know, to understand, and to control, you will increasingly become more able to do so. No one, said Jung, can become conscious of his inner shadows without considerable effort of will, fortitude and moral effort. In the final outcome, the degree of this consciousness will rest in the strength and will of the individual. Like almost any other effort in life, it is ultimately a case of how badly the individual wants what he is after. No one else can give you this "wanting."

3. *Describe Your Shadows:* Recall that we suggested that you record a description of the characters encountered in your dreams, and to do it as soon after awakening as possible. Adequate recording is always a major key to interpretation. You cannot interpret or evaluate what you do not remember. You may not have thought of it before, but every character or figure in your dreams is observable and describable just as is any person you meet in conscious life. The descriptions of these figures are a part of the data that you are gathering for scientific observation. You must have the data, the information with which to work.

A good beginning place is to think of the four conscious functions described in Chapter 2: thinking, feeling, sensation and intuitiveness. As we explained, personality distortion or lopsidedness usually occurs by over- or underdevelopment of one of these functions in the individual. Then what happens within the personality is what Jung called *compensation*—the neglected part of the personality tries to assert itself or to compensate for the neglect. This is also known as the "theory of opposites." That is, the neglected part of the natural personality becomes, in effect, an opposite of the way things really are. Thus, the figures in your dreams often will appear as "personality types" fairly close in description to the four types represented in the four conscious functions. For example, the opposite of the highly rational, thinking personality would be the highly emotional and sensory personality. If the overly-rational person dreams of a very sensory person, it could mean that this neglected side of the personality is trying to express itself. It is trying to change the world (the dreamer's personality) into a replica of itself—which, of course, would also still be one-sided and just as unhealthy as the other-sided or partial personality that already exists. The key in personal adjustment, therefore, is to stop the compensatory force or movement of any side of the personality at the point of equality and balance with the other parts, which also have "rights."

In any case, whichever neglected part of your personality may be trying to assert itself in your dream, as you actually observe that figure and *write down* its characteristics, its nature will become increasingly known to you, and therefore also increasingly easy to handle. The significance of beginning by thinking in terms of the four known main conscious personality types is that as you write descriptions of the shadow figures in your dreams, you will find each emerging as primarily one of the four types. You will see:

— The thinking, perhaps cold and cruel person *or*
— The feeling, nonthinking person *or*
— The sensual, perhaps physically violent or turbulent person *or*
— The intuitive, perhaps phantasmagorical, impulsive and unthinking person

or, you may see any combination or distortion of these four basic functions or types. You may, for example, see the "parent," the "child," or the "adult" within you. You may see the neglected humorous, capricious, or lighthearted side of your nature; or, the mature, sound-thinking, decision-making part of you.

However, what you do with these parts of you,

how you *heed* their assertive behavior becomes another matter. In large measure, they have "done their jobs." They have made themselves known to you. What you have observed and recorded is the natural, self-adjustive attempt of your personality to balance, to individuate itself. And there is a point at which the conscious you must take over and lend a helping hand.

SHADOWS ARE THE SAME SEX

Invariably, a shadow figure seems to be the same sex as the dreamer. This is important as a means of recognition. There are figures of the opposite sex in many dreams. But they usually do not represent the secondary personalities of the dreamer in the sense in which we are speaking here. The reason for the shadow figure being the same sex as the dreamer should be obvious: it *is* the dreamer. The main exception to this is when a person dreams of someone of the same sex with whom he or she has a very close relationship, such as husband, wife, son, daughter, or close friend. Frequently, but not always, these people play themselves in the dream-drama.

There actually are very few people in most dreams, because many of the characters represent the dreamer himself. What the unconscious really does is *use* other people to symbolize parts of itself. What it is saying to the dreamer is that this part of you is *like* this or that person. Technically, this is known as *projection*, which is almost synonymous with the idea of *compensation*, just mentioned. It is the carrying out of the theory of opposites. You unconsciously project the missing or partially lacking aspect of yourself onto a person who has the characteristics that you lack. You identify with that person. In your unconscious, that person becomes a part of your identity, thus compensating for the missing part of your personality.

We might mention in passing that this theory of opposites, this projection or compensation, is what accounts for a corresponding phenomenon in conscious and waking relationships with other people. It is why, for example, people of opposite personality attract and often marry each other. The unconscious exerts a strong influence on the conscious. Nature abhors a void or a vacuum and always tries to fill it. Thus, in your external relationships, you will frequently, instinctively, often unknown to yourself, be attracted to the missing or lacking parts of you that are present in other people. They, in turn, will be attracted in the same way to you. Life is eternally dualistic and polarized. Even the humble magnetized chunk of iron seeks its opposite polarity.

Many of the people in your dreams, when you understand them, turn out to be projections of yourself. Sometimes, even people very close to you can assume such roles in your dreams, especially if they are projections in your conscious life. It thus sometimes requires close observation and *cautious* evaluation to interpret them properly.

MULTIPLE SHADOWS

You can also be thrown off in your interpretation of your own shadow figures by assuming that they may appear one at a time. This is not true. Recall the dream of the man planning to commit the robbery. There were three other people in the dream. *All* were shadow figures. The one who suggested that they might get caught represented the caution, moral side of his character. The other two were not very distinguishable. They seemed to be the silent, "go along with the crowd," follower types—that aspect of the dreamer himself.

SHADOWS ARE NOT ALWAYS NEGATIVE

This is important to reemphasize because there is a natural tendency to think of the unknown, darker sides of one's personality as destructive or discordant. This need not be true, and one should constantly be on the lookout for his "good shadows" too. When you find them, as the young woman found hers in the example dream just cited, listen to their voices. They often are complementary as well as compensatory.

NOT CONFINED TO THE UNCONSCIOUS

The fact that your shadows, your partial or splinter personalities, are not confined solely to your unconscious can be of considerable interpretive help to you. Remember that there is no absolutely clear border dividing the conscious and the unconscious. Your objective observation and evaluation of your own waking behavior can serve as an extension of your dream interpretation efforts. Also, it should be obvious the more that you are aware of in your conscious state, the more aware you will become in your unconscious state, because it is the same mind that does the perceiving and knowing whether asleep or awake.

Practice "stepping outside" yourself while awake. Become an observer of your conscious activity, as you are an observer in your dreams. Learn to observe your own emotional and mental reactions to the people and things around you and the things that happen to you. When you do this while awake, your perceptions and evaluational abilities while sleeping also will improve. All human beings, of course, have a built-in tendency *not* to do this. An objective attitude toward yourself permits a greater chance of a realistic evaluation of what you are and do. As a minimum, constantly seek to clearly see and evaluate (1) What you yourself think and feel, and (2) Your *true* relationships to the people, ideas and feelings that are a part of your waking life. As a result, you will become increasingly capable of a similar evaluation of yourself, the people, the things, and the events in your dreams. There are no hidden, esoteric formulas or potions involved in sound dream interpretation. It is almost entirely a matter of common sense, realism, objective evaluation, and willingness to accept a fact once it is known.

NONHUMAN FIGURES AND SYMBOLS

In addition to people, all dreams have other elements. They have settings, action, movement, inanimate objects, animals, etc. These have significance too. No single volume could list all such possibilities, for they are as many and varied as the people who dream them and the possible experiences of those people. The key to interpreting these, therefore, comes in having a sound theory and set of principles to go by. This is the approach that we urge in this book ... the only sound approach. For, as we have already said, the moment that you start to "look up" this or that symbol, you are completely off the track in your interpretive approach. The beginning point *always* is the life situation and dream content of the dreamer himself. *The prime question always is: What does this mean to the dreamer?*

SUMMARY

In addition to shadow figures, there are other symbolic figures within the personal unconscious which consistently occur in dreams. We will consider these in the next two chapters. An understanding of the shadow figure as just described makes it easier to understand these others. For the moment, if you have grasped the following facts about your shadow figures, you have a good foundation for progressing further into the realm of your own unconscious.

1. Your shadow figures are basically representations of hidden or repressed parts of your own personality.
2. They usually will appear as the same sex as the dreamer.
3. They may, and frequently do, appear in multiple form in a dream.
4. They may be either positive or negative, construction or destructive, complementary or detractive.
5. They also manifest themselves in conscious life.
6. The main keys to recognizing and dealing with them are *sensitivity* to them; willingness to *see, confront* and *embrace* them; and *observation* and *recording* of their characteristics.

Hopefully, you will emerge with a resolution and commitment to do something about your shadow figures once you know them; namely, to integrate them into the rest of your whole personality.

Oh wad some power the giftie gie us
To see oursels as others see us!
It wad frae monie a blunder free us,
An' foolish notion.

Robert Burns

6
The
Outsider

Remember that the figures or images within the unconscious mind are not only "mental pictures." They are actual personalities. The main thing that they are lacking is a body through which to perform, to carry out their tendencies and desires for expression. They are just as much *persons* as is your conscious self. They are active and behavior-influencing personalities. They do things in both the conscious and unconscious worlds.

In addition to our inner personalities or shadow selves each of us actually has not one but many outer or conscious selves. That is, even at the conscious level we are more than one person. Metaphorically speaking, each of us wears many masks and plays many roles in conscious life.

Some psychologists call these masks that we wear in conscious life *functional complexes.* As we explained, a complex is basically a method of behavior and reaction that a person develops in order to deal with a given set of circumstances in his life. Or, a complex may be merely a grouping of ideas or associations within the inner being of a person. Complexes per se usually are associated with conflict and emotion. They usually are repressed. And, they usually represent *escape* methods of dealing with things that we cannot cope with in conscious life. This is why psychotherapy aims to get complexes into the open where they can be dealt with in a realistic way, instead of hiding from them and continuing to repress them.

The functional complex, however, is of a different kind, although it still can get us into trouble if it is not properly integrated and accepted as a part of the whole personality. Jung called functional complexes *personas* after the Latin term *personae* for the characters in a play or drama. This is precisely what our functional complexes amount to. Life is a drama in which each individual is called upon to play many roles. We learn to do this from childhood. The child, for example, soon learns in life that in order to get along in the home with his parents and brothers and sisters, he is expected to "perform" in a certain way—whether or not that behavior is what his *real* inner drives and impulses want to do and be. As he grows older and goes to school, he learns to wear other masks in order to please his teacher, the policeman on the street, the clerk in the store, or his peers. As he continues into adult life, he learns to wear all the other masks that various phases of society require of him in order to function and be accepted. Many of these roles, or the masks that represent them—his persona—ultimately will become quite complex and involved. At home, one persona will predominate; in church another; on the job yet another. He will have still others for passing friends and intimate associates. If he gets into a profession, still other roles will be required of him. If he becomes a doctor or a psychiatrist, for example, he will be required to behave in an extra-mature way in handling other people's problems—*and their personas*. But he will still have his real self as well.

Your personas thus may be quite normal and serve useful functions in life. Many of them are parts of the personality that develop to govern and control the behavior necessary to meet the everyday requirements of life. They keep us compatible with other human beings. There is, however, a danger. Your personas are rarely the real you. And that "you" still needs its rightful and proper share of life. The danger is that if you allow any single persona to take over and to usurp those needs, tension and inner conflict, even neuroses, may develop. For what you will be doing is denying your real self and *its* normal needs and requirements. You will be denying the validity and rights of other parts of your whole self. Your self-adjustive, psychic mechanism will not long permit this, and one of the first manifestations of its attempt to assert and adjust itself is likely to occur in a dream. An example will illustrate this. A business executive in his forties dreamed the following:

> I had dozed on the sofa in my den on a Saturday afternoon. In my dream, I was in bed with my wife when I became quite vividly aware that there was a burglar drying to break into a basement window. I jumped out of bed and ran downstairs and into a storage room. In this room, on shelves running near the window, I keep several boxes labeled "family keepsakes," containing various special toys from the children's early childhood and sentimental items such as the first pictures they drew at school, my teenage daughter's five-year-old handprint in plaster of paris that she made for me in the first grade, etc. The burglar is at the window over the shelves, still trying to get in. I notice, however, that the contents of the boxes are already strewn about, and particularly take note of the little handprint mold lying on top of the papers. I remember wondering how these things became disarrayed when the burglar had not yet entered. Somehow I manage to bar or fasten the window as the intruder still struggles to get in. I see his face. It is familiar, but I cannot identify him. He goes to another window. I hurry to bar it and succeed. But he keeps going from window to window, determined to break in.

> The next thing I know, he is at the kitchen door. I rush upstairs, but too late. As I run in frightened panic toward the door, it crashes open, and I almost smack into him as he stands ready to enter and grab me. I scream and awaken.

At first glance, this might appear to be just another shadow dream. In a way, it is. For the unconscious also bears within it images of the persona that are very similar to shadow figures. Sometimes a persona dream may be confused with a shadow dream. Both types of figures behave very much alike in the unconscious. There is no real harm in this confusion, since the real aim of interpretation remains the same: to *recognize* any part of the personality that either needs attention—or is getting more than its share of the whole being. In either case, the figure represents an opposite, or at least a partial opposite, of the way things presently are in the dreamer's personality.

Again, we must know something of the total psychic situation of the dreamer. Briefly, he is a career department manager in a large, sales-oriented corporation for which he began working eighteen years ago as a salesman and worked up to a management position. As in most such organizations, much stress is placed on "maintaining the right image," dedication to the job, and identifying with the company goals. In other words, a certain rather complex persona is required. Being a second-line manager, Henry not only preaches these things to his subordinates, but they have also come to have great importance as a part of his acquired makeup. He still spends long hours at the office in trying to live up to those standards, and this particular Saturday at home is itself a rarity for him. Looking at his larger life, Henry is, at heart, a sensitive, conscientious and humanitarian person. All of his instincts, as they say, are "in the right place," but there "just never seems to be enough time to do everything that should be done."

What has happened to Henry is that his persona, his mask, has almost become *him*—his whole conscious self. He has shut his real self out, a common occurrence among men of his status. The figure and symbols in his dream are almost self-explanatory. The "intruder" whose face he knows but cannot identify is none other than the neglected part or parts of him trying to "get back in." And it should be obvious why the sentimental mementos of perhaps happier times are already disturbed. The intruder has not ransacked them. He, or what he has become, has done this.

Many people in present-day society over-identify with their personas in this way. (Have you?) The energy necessary just to fulfill the roles they are playing leaves little room for real living. This particular man, incidentally, has had many similar dreams. Always, there is someone "trying to get in" or to "intrude." We know that these figures are not really intruders at all, but parts of his personality seeking their rightful place in his total being. It is also sad that this dreamer, as do many, still dismisses his dreams as "merely dreams," and gives them little or no serious thought as a possible basis for corrective action in his life. The dreams actually were reported to us by his wife who has become increasingly concerned at their recurrence and consistency—and with a deteriorating family relationship.

The same sort of occurrence is not uncommon in children and can lead to lasting personality damage. Take, for example, the child of whom an adult persona is required too early in life. This often occurs as a result of unavoidable economic circumstances. But parents also can be responsible. Again, a certain amount of imitation of and identification with adults is desirable in the life of a child. This is a major way that we all learn and grow. But when too much is required of a child too soon, the impact and results will invariably be felt in later life.

One example of this is a 23-year-old woman whom we have known since childhood. This person was raised with both her mother and her grandmother present in the home, and at least partially under the influence of her great-grandmother. In so many ways, as we watched her grow up, we were aware that she was not being allowed to be simply a child. From almost the moment that she could think she was taught her "responsibilities": never to miss choir rehearsal; never to offend; that "proper Christian ladies" do not display their emotions; in short, the entire matriarchal, Bible-belt mentality that has ruined many a young woman like her. Her family's motives undoubtedly were above reproach. But through a combination of environment and circumstances, Marie was—for all intents and purposes—robbed of her childhood.

Observe this young woman today. She has never had a normal relationship with a young man. Since grammar school, she has been an "A" student and consistently made the dean's list in college. Just finishing now, she will graduate with honors. The life-work she has chosen is to be a missionary and to work with little children, deprived children—of whom she often dreams. Undoubtedly, this is an admirable calling, but at what needless cost is it a compensation for her own loss of normal childhood? This, incidentally, often is one of the paradoxes of compensation in the human personality. It frequently does lead to outstanding achievement through the adjustive effort. But the trade-off is terribly great in terms of one-sided personalities and lives that remain unfulfilled in so many other aspects. The adult person too often winds up with no identity of his own, no true sense of self, or as the psychologists say, no "ego-consciousness." He literally is someone else.

What can be done? If you are a parent, you can see that you do not require too much of the wrong thing too soon in your own child's life. If you yourself are not sure of which one of your personas is really you, you can start now to find out. You may be able to find out through your dreams, if you listen to what they have to say to you. Then, you can recognize your personas for what they are. Accept them as normal parts of you. But do not permit them to take over. You may want to eliminate some undesirable persona, but more likely you will want to embrace these other parts of you and *integrate* them into the rest of you—*never forgetting who and what you really are*. Do not make your self the outsider. Learn to consciously let down your masks in your own thinking and to give the real you a chance to express itself.

A woman impudent and mannish grown
Is not more loath'd than an effeminate man.

William Shakespeare
Troilus and Cressida
Act II; Scene 2

7

The Man and Woman Within

There is another important aspect of the human personality that has a direct bearing upon the contents and interpretation of dreams. This has to do with certain psychological factors in men and women. Some psychologists still see no difference in the psychological makeups of men and women. Jung was concerned with the problem and advanced the idea that in every man there is an opposite, female side to his personality; and in every woman there is an opposite, male side to her personality. From what we now know about human personality, this idea seems to have much credibility.

Much psychological teaching in the earlier part of this century almost totally ignored the possibility of significant psychological differences in men and women. It is only lately, and largely under the influence of the writings of Jung, that the distinction is coming to be taken into account. Interestingly, the idea that in every man there is some woman, and in every woman some man, has been around for a long time. One reads in the Adam and Eve story in the Bible how woman was taken out of man. One reads in various early mythological accounts of how daughters sprang from the heads of their fathers. Plato, for example, wrote how originally human beings were androgynous (that is, united as one sex). All beings, he said, had two faces, four hands, four feet, and were double in every other way. They also were spherical in shape, signifying wholeness. These male-female beings, according to the legend, assaulted the gods, and Zeus, the father of the gods, split them in two. Since then, they have striven and longed to be reunited.

Can there be any doubt that woman completes man; that man completes woman? Together, they are a whole. Man springs from woman, and places his seed back within a woman to make other men and women. The body of the male contains female characteristics, the most notable being breasts corresponding in structure to those of the female; so also does the woman carry indications of maleness, such as the clitoris which corresponds to the male penis.

The question, therefore, is not whether men and women have inherent opposite sexual sides. It is whether these sides manifest themselves only at the physical level or at both the physical and psychological levels. There seems little doubt that the latter is true, through simple observation by even the layman. What man does not at times behave psychologically like a woman, and what woman does not behave like a man on occasion? Some men, in fact, behave more like women than men, and vice versa.

In a man, the psychological representation of his opposite sexual aspect is known as the *anima*. In a woman, it is known as the *animus*. The terms, with their feminine and masculine endings, derive from a Latin word meaning "soul," "spirit," or "breath of life." It might be said that a man's anima lies closer to the center of his psychic being than any other force except his basic being as a man. Even his heart has two beats—the diastolic and systolic. Psychically speaking, his anima is like the second beat of his heart. It is like the second pulse of an alternating electrical current. The same applies to woman in reverse.

Each man and woman seemingly inherits a predisposition, perhaps a "psychic embryo," for his and her anima and animus, respectively, as a fundamental, secondary part of his and her personality. Recall the description of shadow figures, complexes, and splinter personalities. The anima and animus behave in a way very similar to these. The anima and animus are similar in that they also (1) Manifest themselves in conscious behavior, and (2) Appear in the unconscious and in dreams as *figures*. In the conscious behavior of men, for example, it is the anima that causes behavior normally associated with females, such as moodiness, illogical and irrational behavior on occasion, poutiness, peevishness, etc. In a woman, the conscious manifestations of her animus may range from taking a typically male opinionated stand on a subject to the uttering of meaningless slogans and idealistic phrases, blustering, strutting, etc. What man has not, for example, been accused of acting like a "bitchy female" on occasion; or, what woman has not been accused of being "hard as nails"? Most such behavior is a manifestation of the anima or animus.

Like other aspects of the human personality, the anima and animus express themselves in our unconscious largely through the medium of dreams. They express themselves in a variety of forms, depending on what characteristics they possess and their state within the individual person. As might also be expected, like other aspects of the human personality, the anima and animus can exist in a healthy or unhealthy state. They can be allowed to grow and mature with the rest of the personality. They can be permitted to express themselves in a natural way as a part of the total person. Or, they may be unnaturally repressed, not allowed their natural and rightful places as parts of the balanced and homogeneous total personality. If the latter is the case in a person, they invariably will make themselves known in a self-adjustive effort to compensate. They will do this at both the conscious and the unconscious levels. They can do this in either a destructive or constructive way. Much depends on how well they are observed and interpreted.

THE STATE OF YOUR SOUL

Dreams in which the anima or animus appear are frequently known as soul dreams, because they represent the "second nature" of a person. Like shadow figures, the anima and animus have no bodies of their own. They exist primarily as unconscious images. They always exist in a certain state within each individual, and the unconscious image takes on the characteristics of that state. If, for example, a man's female side has never been permitted to develop beyond its primitive stage, this is the way that it will appear in his unconscious, in dreams. The form in which it appears might be described as a good representation of the "state of his soul." In the actual dream of one young woman, for example, her animus appeared recurrently in the literal shape of a huge, man-sized penis. Upon analysis, it became quite clear that this was precisely the level to which the natural male side of her personality had been allowed to develop. Largely through the influence of her parents and several unfortunate incidents in her childhood, her natural maleness had been repressed. Her male side, in effect, had never grown beyond the purely sensual level. To her inner self, this was exactly what a man was, nothing but a big p----. Her unconscious image of manhood, built from the information that her conscious perceptions provided, had never been permitted to accumulate data about the more refined characteristics of maleness, of the intelligent, sensitive and aesthetic, as well as the sensual, full-fledged, whole mature male. When her male side tried to assert and express itself it did so in terms of the impressions provided by her experience.

It should be reemphasized here that when we speak of "figures in the unconscious" we always speak of images within the mind, and that these images are formed largely from information received through the conscious functions. The unconscious starts out in its development with what at best might be described as a predisposition to become composed of certain images. That is, there probably is merely a primordial form, a nascent instinct upon which the image will be built. But the building process itself invariably is a result of consciously perceived information— or the lack of consciously perceived information. Almost all personality growth and development seem to be a result of this process or some shortcoming or breakdown in what it was intended to be.

Unlike shadow figures, which appear in dreams in the same sex as the dreamer, the anima and the animus appear as figures of the opposite sex—because they *are* of the opposite sex. They are not too difficult to recognize in your dreams. Generally speaking, when you dream of a person of the opposite sex, it is well to consider the possibility of its being an anima or animus figure. The main exception is the same as for shadow figures. Usually, people with whom you have close relationships in conscious life appear as themselves. There is another exception to this also. This is when the person of whom you dream may be a *projection* of your opposite side. Projection is the transference of the characteristics of a figure within one's own unconscious onto another person. That is, a person sometimes can actually see his or her own anima or animus (or at least part of it) walking around in a living human body other than his or her own. As already mentioned, in order to fulfill their deep, often compulsive craving for wholeness, a man or woman frequently will marry his or her anima or animus figure. It is quite common for a man to "fall in love" with that woman who most closely approximates a missing or underdeveloped part of his own femaleness. There are many examples of this in novels and literature, as well as in real life. Where the external study and cure fail, the internal, self-adjustive, wholeness-seeking *nature* of man and woman will still continue in its seeking and striving toward wholeness. Thus, although we may dream of specific people, they do not necessarily portray themselves. They may quite likely be projections of parts of us, often the missing parts of us, with which our unconscious identifies.

Remember, too, that your dreams are highly personal and subjective experiences. There is not as great a variety of characters in them as it may at first seem. It can safely be said that the majority of human figures (and some of the inanimate objects as well) in your dreams are representations of parts of you. Many of the people may be different figures or representations for the same character—you.

The anima and the animus, like shadow figures, do not always appear in a *single* figure. They may appear in multiple forms, in the same or different dreams. Much depends upon what the unconscious "decides" is the most accurate representation or image with which to portray that part of itself that it is trying to express at a given time. In addition, the anima and animus do not always appear in human form. The representation could just as well be in the form of an animal, or even something inanimate such as a house. In one man's dream, his anima appeared as a vicious female animal; in another, a gentle cow. And the same man had both of these dreams. It is very interesting that, for some reason within his personality, both representations were animals, although different kinds of animals. We do know that animals represent, among other things, unthinking sensuality. And this may be a clue. To interpret these particular dreams, one would, however, have to know something of the larger life of this man, including what these animals meant to him. It is certain that he definitely has something "animalistic" within him and that this animalism definitely is female. And since animals do exist largely at the sensual level, there are some grounds to suppose that this man has a female sensuality within his unconscious which ranges between viciousness and bovineness.

In any case, once you have identified a figure in your dream as an anima or animus figure, and observed its characteristics, you will have a fairly accurate image of the state of the opposite sexual side of your personality. You will see to what extent this natural opposite sexual side of you has developed and matured. If it is in an unhealthy, distorted, unfulfilled or dysfunctioning state, it will so express itself. If, on the other hand, it is receiving its due recognition and opportunity for expression within a balanced, mature, total personality, it will appear as such. If, in fact, the latter is the case, it may not appear at all. For it already is appearing and expressing itself as a normal part of your life. It is a fairly general truism in all dream interpretation that figures do not appear unless they are "having a problem."

THE ANIMA

Let us consider briefly the normal functioning of the female side of a man as a basis for recognition and observation of its image in a dream. Every male comes into life already equipped with his anima, or at least a predisposition for the development of a female aspect.

From this point on, how this other side of his nature develops is largely a function of his relationships with actual women. For the first couple of years of his life, there is hardly any distinction as to whether he is a boy or a girl, the biggest difference probably being the colors in which his mother dresses him. He has the same contacts with the female body of his mother that a girl has. Boy and girl alike suckle and snuggle at the female breast. In his dawning conscious and unconscious, a female image thus begins to sheath and encase his already existing femininity.

Remember that much (although not all) of what is unconscious was once consciously perceived and later stored away. This is where the information storage process begins. Obviously, at this very embryonic stage, these early impressions, which can never be forgotten, are not simply recorded. They have a formative influence. What the child sees and experiences in these early years will have a lasting influence. The kind of woman that his mother is, therefore, imprints upon his unconscious an indelible image of what his own femaleness ought to be. But because he is primarily a male, also established is a *relationship* between his own maleness and both his inner femaleness and external femaleness in general. The latter is represented first by his mother and is gradually expanded as he develops relationships with other females. Gradually, throughout the growing years, and often on into adult life, one of two basic things can happen to his inherent femaleness. It can *overdevelop* at the expense of his primary masculinity. Or, it can *underdevelop* at its own expense.

Suppose, for example, that a mother is overly affectionate and demonstrative toward her son. During infancy and early childhood, this is quite normal. But in later life it is not, because it restricts the natural development of other relationships. It is normal for a mother to become less important to her son as life goes on.

Usually, in mis-development there also is a general downgrading of masculinity. If the son becomes more important to the mother than the father, the son will see his father, and therefore masculinity, as of secondary importance in the scheme of things. He will learn to admire femininity more than masculinity. What life is really telling him is that femaleness is more important and desirable than maleness, and this image becomes implanted in his unconscious and superimposes itself over his already existing, female side. The same sort of thing happens when the male influence is lacking, for example, when a mother is widowed and does not remarry. This is the classic "mother complex." Often, it develops into sexual perversion.

Suppose, on the other hand, that femaleness is downgraded. This undoubtedly happens more frequently in our society. A male child, for example, may repeatedly be admonished that "men don't cry," "men are hard and strong," "men don't show their emotions," "don't do this or that thing" that is distinctly feminine. The opposite then occurs in the development of what should be a perfectly natural side of his personality. The boy's anima will be repressed, shoved down into his unconscious, out of sight and hearing. It will be stunted in its growth, and the image that is implanted upon his unconscious will be a less than normal or healthy one. His anima will still try to assert and express itself, but it will do so in the form of what it is, because it must "work" with the information available to it. If it is still a child, it probably will appear in his dreams as a child. If his femininity is still in its primitive, animalistic state, it will manifest itself as such.

We should reemphasize here that things within the unconscious are not nearly so cut-and-dried as they may appear on the printed page. For, in all probability, any man's femininity, his anima, and its corresponding unconscious image representation are splintered and multiple, just as are the shadow aspects of his personality. Within him, there are no doubt several, often conflicting, conceptions of his own feminine aspect. At one time it may appear, for example, as a peevish figure, giving vent to poutiness or distinctively feminine irritability. At another time, it may appear in a mature and motherly form. And, of course, because the influence can occur at *either the conscious or unconscious level*, he may actually act out a given role in waking life.

Regardless, however, of what form the anima takes, in either a dream or in conscious life, the whole point and aim remains one of establishing harmony and wholeness. The normal, mature male does not repress his female side. He feels no embarrassment or guilt in allowing the gentler, more intuitive, more compassionate side of his nature to display itself in his conscious life. When he does this, that nature will remain in a harmonious state in his inner, unconscious self as well. Even his occasional female-like irrational or illogical moods will be taken in stride. He will have a good relationship with the woman within, and consequently with the women in his external life as well, largely because he has not selected them to compensate for something he is lacking, but upon their own merits and standing as females. Such a man is unlikely to have very many dreams in which his anima is trying to assert itself. When he does have anima dreams, they will probably not be of a traumatic nature. Such a man is rare in our society.

THE ANIMUS

Generally speaking, the development of a healthy animus in the personality of a woman follows a pattern similar to that of the anima in the man. It begins with a girl's experience and identification with her father and grows with the various inputs received from observation and interaction with other men. Most women are more fortunate than men in that, overall, their opposite sexual sides seem to be better integrated into their total personalities than are men's. This undoubtedly is largely attributable to the fact that it is not as difficult for a woman in our society to behave in an inconsistent way as it is for a man. Women are expected to fluctuate in mood and temperament anyway. Therefore, not as much attention is called to their variations in behavior, including the male aspects of their behavior. Women in our society tend to be "goddess figures" to men, and their behavior is accepted and tolerated.

One of the best ways to observe an unhealthy animus in a woman is to note her competitiveness with men. Usually, the consistently argumentative woman also has an animus problem, as does the woman with a lack of sensitivity or compassion for the feelings of others. Most women's liberation extremists probably have an animus problem. On the other hand, men with no psychological knowledge quickly become aware of the woman whose animus is neither underdeveloped nor overdeveloped. She has the quality of being a woman, with all of the charm and tenderness of the female. Yet, she also stands on her own two feet with dignity and just the right amount of self-sufficiency and conviction in her opinions. She, incidentally, needs no "liberation" for she already is free in the only place that counts—inside herself.

Most of the other things said about the development of the male anima also apply to the development of the female animus. Lack of a father figure altogether, or the presence of a weak or less than desirable father, has the same effect in reverse. Women, too, are just as likely to be attracted to their opposite or missing parts.

SUMMARY

There are at least four important clues that will give you some indication as to whether or not a figure in your dreams may be an anima or animus figure. These are as follows:

1. If it is of the opposite sex
2. If it is not a person of close relationship
3. If, in the man's dream, it displays a distinctive set of characteristics, such as peevishness, bitchiness, sensuality, immaturity—or, on the positive side, maturity, gentleness, motherliness, etc.
4. If, in the woman's dream, it displays characteristics of arbitrariness, insensitivity, mechanistic or aggressive behavior—or, on the positive side, decisiveness, protectiveness, etc.

Remember, too, that we are not necessarily saying that qualities such as "bitchiness" in the female, or "blustering" in the male, are inherited. What we are saying is that they are inherent in our social structure and therefore form the information available to the unconscious in its perception and development. We do not want to be accused of being "male chauvinist pigs."

8
The
Collective Unconscious

Some thinkers contend that the human mind, or psyche, comes into this world as a total blank and that everything stored within it is a result of some experience or activity in its present lifetime. The investigation of dreams and other aspects of the unconscious indicates that this may not be so. There seems to be more within the psychological makeup of an individual than merely that which his conscious and unconscious accumulate during his own lifetime, perhaps an inherited substratum already present when a person is born. This substratum Jung called the *collective unconscious*. The deeper one goes into the psyche the more do the contents of the unconscious seem to lose their individual uniqueness and become universalized—common to all men. Thus, at its very "bottom," the psyche becomes simply "human nature" or "human being." The term collective unconscious suits this deeper stratum of the psyche for two reasons. First, it is a collection of mental instincts and predispositions which at the lower level border on and merge at some unknown point with the physiological, and at the upper level with the personal unconscious. Second, it is collective with respect to man in the sense of its commonness to all men.

Through the medium of genes and chromosomes, it can, in a sense, be said that man "remembers" from generation to generation. Each of us, for example, inherits the same propensity to walk upright that our forebears developed. Through combinations of our genes and chromosomes, the units of physical memory, our bodies reproduce certain eye colors, body builds and longevity characteristics, even predispositions to certain diseases. Each of us somehow "remembers" to be drawn to members of the opposite sex, to make and perpetuate the species. Even the hairs on the backs of our necks prickle when we are frightened or angry, just as those of our great, great grandfathers and their grandfathers before them did.

Is it not possible also that every individual may be endowed with certain mental instincts and propensities, such as the anima and animus, which we have already discussed. True, some of these instincts seem to border, at their lower levels, upon the physiological. But at some unknown or ill-defined place in our makeups, they merge with our psychic or psychological beings. For example, all of us have a natural herding instinct, or gregariousness, a need to belong to a group. Doubtless, this drive connects at its root to our physiological need to perpetuate the species. But there is more to our need to be together than sex and survival. Over the eons, what may have begun as a mere physiological urge has developed into a *social imperative*. Perhaps a psychic evolution, similar to physical evolution, has occurred. There are other such imperatives. Humans have, for example, what seems to be an instinctive urge to be pugnacious toward each other, to compete and fight with one another. This is paradoxical and at odds, of course, with the gregarious motive. We are dualistic and

contradictory beings in many ways. Doubtless, our pugnacity evolved in a way similar to our gregariousness,
perhaps out of a self-defense need, or is related to our
inherent need for individual autonomy. Another interesting
imperative is what seems to be the instinctive drive and
need for order and structure within all humans. Place a
human being in any environment and he will almost
immediately strive to "arrange" it in some way—usually in
a circle with himself at the center. All of these imperatives,
and others, are a part of the collective unconscious.

Nor does the unconscious contain only psycho-
physiological instincts. Analysis indicates that it also
harbors predispositions to produce certain *ideas and
thought patterns.* Do not confuse the *predisposition* to
produce certain ideas with ideas per se. The human mind
does not inherit ideas themselves, merely the inclination to
form ideas. This is a different matter entirely from that of
the physiological instinct, say, of sex or mating. It is
different, also, from the emotional or sociological instincts
such as fear, pugnacity or gregariousness. It may be related
to such imperatives as the need for order and structure,
which is more refined than herding or aggressiveness, and
yet less refined than other needs. This predisposition to
produce images and ideas is probably more closely related
to the fantasy, daydreaming and combinatory creativity
described earlier. It is a definite propensity to produce
mental ideas as opposed to mere behavioral patterns.

For example, in addition to all his other imperatives,
since his earliest existence, man has both feared the unknown and experienced an affinity with it. He has sought
wholeness, unity, rectitude and harmony. Deep within his
being, perhaps even touching a physiological, chemical
craving to be reunited with the original elements from
which he was taken, dwells an imperative to make contact
with the original creative force, whoever or whatever it was:

Deep within him, also, is the capability to make symbols to represent this experience. Some may presume that man created the "God idea." But the psychic energy within man that was ultimately the imperative, that was ultimately the idea, that was ultimately the symbol, that was finally the spoken and written idea of God, might have preexisted within him. As consciousness and language evolved, man simply became better able to articulate his imperatives, first representing them in crude symbols and later in myths and stories. "Before Abraham was, I am," said God in the Biblical articulation. It took a long time to get to this point. The Biblical story, or the myth, such as the Garden of Eden or the Cain and Abel story, may not have happened as an historical event at a specific time, but it may have happened simply because it contains a hint of what may have happened to man.

Early philosophers groped with this idea of inherited imperatives in numerous ways. It was not until the time of Jung, however, that serious thought was given to it. After all, it represents a "marriage" of the philosophical (even the religious) with scientific "objectivism." And these fields have had a running feud since the Enlightenment. Jung identified these imperatives or primordial energies—nucleuses, as it were, out of which ideas might evolve—as *archetypes*. He was able to identify them largely through a combination of the following factors:

1. The interpretation of thousands of individual dreams
2. Study of man's present psychological makeup
3. Study of man's psychiatric history
4. Study of man's intellectual history and evolution and the recurring themes in them

In empirically examining the dreams of numerous patients, Jung was repeatedly struck by a significant illuminating observation. The material in some dreams clearly *could not be associated with or related to any known personal experience of the person who dreamed it.* In other words, the hypothesis did not hold that *all* of the contents of the human mind, conscious or unconscious, are a result of something that he has personally experienced. Certain dreams produced some material that clearly had not been "put into" the mind of the dreamer during his lifetime. Presumably, according to most psychiatrists, the human conscious and unconscious (or, memory, if one wishes), are one-way receptors. That is, there supposedly is only one way for their stored images, memories, impressions, etc., no matter how complex or deeply hidden, to get stored in them. This would be through the personal experiencing of those data at *some* time or place in the actual life of the individual. If this is true, it means that every dream relates to something that a person has actually experienced. But this does not seem always to be the case. Some dreams *do not* relate to the personal experience of the dreamer.

Some of the most convincing evidence of this comes from the recorded dreams of children, although it is not limited to children. Children proved to be particularly useful in this study, as opposed to older people, because their limited exposure in life makes it relatively easy to determine whether or not they have had previous access to the material in their dreams.

From his studies, Jung hypothesized that certain dreams arise spontaneously out of the unconscious, from the inherited, collective memory of mankind. He called these dreams *archetypal dreams* because when interpreted they bore a remarkable similarity to some of the imperatives that man has recurrently expressed throughout the ages, particularly in the form of symbols, myths, legends and religious stories. Many times, for example, dreamers see in their dream symbols or other images never actually seen in their lives. When these images and symbols have been described, drawn, and investigated, they have in many cases turned out to be near or perfect duplicates of symbols and images recorded long ago in myths, in legends, as religious idols, on the walls of ancient tombs, etc.

One of the most interesting aspects of the archetypal dream is its similarity to mythology. Until the time of Jung, with a few isolated exceptions, modern thinkers tended to relegate myths to the realm of meaningless and useless fantasy, at best to the efforts of primitive and earlier man to express in anthropomorphic terms the unexplainable natural phenomena in his environment. This point of view is partially true. But there also is a large body of mythology that expressed certain life experiences long before modern science, and often more accurately than "objective" data observation might permit.

The simple truth is that modern man is not as far removed from primitive man in the experiencing of the universals of life as some thinkers would have us believe. In psychic and emotional makeup, twentieth century man is no more than a hairsbreadth away from his earliest known and recorded primitive civilized counterpart. Evolution— physical and psychological—moves very slowly. In the heart of every modern man or woman beats the pulse of all the fears of the unknown, the cruelties of the most primitive aggressiveness, as well as the yearnings and searchings for connection with the infinite. Strip modern man of his technology and his thin veneer of socialization and civilization—within a matter of hours, days at the most, he will revert to his simplistic, primitive self. He will be no different from his neolithic brother. For, within the world of his deeper unconscious, he is still the same.

THE COLLECTIVE IN THE CONSCIOUS WORLD

The principle that the unconscious influences and manifests itself in the conscious world carries through here in speaking of the collective unconscious experience. Dreams, of course, remain as the most available and observable manifestations of what we are experiencing in our inner, unconscious worlds. We shall consider these in the next section. For the moment, however, let us look at how the inherited, collective experience of mankind manifests itself in our conscious world. This also will shed additional light upon how it reveals itself in our dreams. To do both of these things, it is necessary to understand the meaning and the use of the term *archetype*.

Many English words begin with the prefix, *arch*, *arche*, or *archi*, which derives from the Greek *archein* which means "the first" or "the original." The root *typos* means "form" or "pattern." Anything that is archetypal, therefore, is "of or related to the original pattern," or a duplicate of it. The anima and the animus, for example, are predispositions after which each individual person is patterned. Naturally, they manifest themselves both consciously and unconsciously. The animus and anima are not the only archetypes within us. We have already alluded to another: the God archetype, or the God imperative, or the God image, or simply, the wholeness imperative. Any of these terms will do.

The God archetype is one of the easiest to follow throughout the *arch*eological development of man. It has always been present in human culture, and it is undoubtedly the most pervasive of all cultural archetypes. By tracing its development, we can see the nature of other archetypes and how they have developed and been expressed. Another way of saying this is that the God archetype has always been present in man.

It is quite conceivable that primitive man's first awareness of the Divine, Creative Force was merely fright and anticipation, perhaps a mere instinct or awareness. It took man several million years to reach the point where he actually would articulate what he "knew"—within his most primitive thoughts—to be true. It took him perhaps another million or so years before he could draw his first crude symbols for what his "bones cried out to be true." The careful thinker, by the way, will see no contradiction here with the traditional ideas of God as recorded in sacred writings. The contrary is true. These ideas gain a new and deeper meaning from this interpretation. One suddenly sees, for example, the true depth of meaning in such Biblical passages as the following:

> And the Lord God formed man . . . and breathed into his nostrils the breath of life; and man became a *living soul.*
> *Genesis 2:7*

> The heavens declare the glory of God; and the firmament sheweth his handiwork.
> *Psalms 19:1*

> . . . one day is with the Lord as a thousand years, and a thousand years as one day.
> *2 Peter 3:8*

> [*God*] having made known unto us the mystery of his will, according to his good pleasure which he has purposed in himself: that in the dispensation of the fulness of times he might gather together in one all things . . .
> *Ephesians 1:9-10*

> . . . the spirit maketh intercession for us with groanings that cannot be uttered.
> *Romans 8:25*

These were no mere off-the-cuff mutterings of primitive writers. They actually are highly refined statements of perception and thought. And it should be noted that Dr. Jung, who spent a lifetime examining these matters in depth, when asked if he believed in God, answered: "Believe? No, I do not believe; *I know*."

Another interesting observation can be made here. This is that most archetypes are cross-cultural. That is, the *same* fundamental human experiences can be found among almost all human civilizations regardless of geographical separation or distance. Archeologists and anthropologists have long been aware of this, and have found much evidence of the commonness of the collective human experience. It would take considerable time and space to outline even the best known of these commonalities. Notable examples include the similarities between the Egyptian and Mayan calendars, the repeated recurrence of certain symbols such as the circle, the mandala, the cross, etc., in all cultures. Other similarities include the mythologies and legends of various cultures. For example, almost every culture has a legend about an early age of peace, rectitude and wholeness such as the Biblical Garden of Eden. Many divergent cultures have legends of a flood or inundation similar to the Biblical account. Almost every culture has a legend of a semidivine hero such as Christ or Prometheus, who stole fire from the gods. Similarly there are the various stories of the godlike trickster figure such as the Norse Loki, or Pan. The American Indians also had their figure. Then there is the human experience of dualism as epitomized in the Greek Gemini twins, Castor and Pollux, the Cain and Abel story, the tale of Romulus and Remus, founders of Rome, and the Sons of the Sun of certain American Indian tribes. There is, of course, the universal human experience of motherhood and femininity as epitomized in "mother earth," the ancient goddess Astarte, the Virgin Mary, etc. Only a careful and detailed study would reveal all of these collective experiences and their similarities.

Another example is the universal experience of childhood. Everyone was himself once a baby and a child and *knows* within himself the experiences of newness, inferiority, the craving for love and attention, the simplicity and straightforwardness represented in babyhood and childhood.

But man also collectively experiences his childhood, his smallness and dependency in relation to the universe and the forces it contains. "Unless you become as a little child, you shall not see the kingdom of heaven," Jesus admonished, and "A little child shall lead them." These are articulations of this archetypal relationship and experience. Repeatedly throughout history, man has expressed his "child experience." His religious legends begin with accounts of it. The stories of the founding of his cities and nations relate to it. The tales of his great exoduses often begin with it. Even his gods and heroes are first pictured as babies or children.

Similarly, the experience of motherhood and fatherhood must be regarded as archetypal. So must the experience of birth and death—and the hope of resurrection. Even some animals, for instance, the cat and the serpent, represent archetypes. These, too, are symbolic of collective experiences. The elements, such as earth, air, fire and water, also represent archetypal experiences and actually have been used as symbols for such. Water, for example, is a very interesting symbolic expression for an inner experience of man. It is also the basis for the letter "m" in the alphabet. It is deep and dark. Its depths are mysterious, as are the depths of man's own unconscious. It moves and flows. It refreshes and sustains. Ultimately, it may even swallow and engulf. It is a safe assumption that if a person dreams of water, some or all of these symbolic recollections may be present. In dreams, water is often representative of the unconscious itself.

Another interesting archetype is what Jung called the "wise old man archetype." Like the God archetype, it may have begun as merely an awareness, fear or anticipation and later evolved into symbolic representations. For many centuries, at least a part of that symbolism has been anthropomorphic. That is, the symbology representing the "God image" within man has been man himself—"having the form of man," which is what the term "anthropomorphic" means. "God created man, and man promptly returned Him the compliment," is how one nineteenth century writer put it. This, of course, has always been a part of our problem in comprehending God as a force—or as a spiritual personality. We tend to use man as the basis for understanding God. In any case, deep within each of us there is a "wise old man," something or someone representing the creative wisdom of the ages, so to speak. Dreaming of such a character could thus be an archetypal expression.

MAN AND HIS SYMBOLS

Man's earliest conscious expression of his unconscious archetypal images took the form of simple symbols. The oldest of these is undoubtedly the circle. Most people see dozens of circular shapes and symbols every day without realizing that a great many of them actually are articulations of man's most fundamental archetypal experience. Among other things, the circle is at once a most simplistic and most profound statement. It is found in every ancient and modern culture. The circle, in all probability, was the first articulation of the God archetype. It is the symbol of the wholeness and unity that man feels drawn toward. It extends outward in every direction from its center. It can be conceived to include everything, all existence, within its outer boundaries. It symbolizes both the finite and the infinite since it both encloses and has no beginning and no ending. The circle is both abstract and concrete. It symbolizes not only the wholeness of the universe, but the wholeness and completeness of the human psyche as well. Throughout history, the circle, or mandala, has been believed to have divine or magical properties. The ancient

Hindu dieties were arranged in a mandala. The Chinese Book of Changes, the I Ching, by which Chinese leaders purportedly governed for thousands of years, is based upon eight trigrams representing life arranged in a circle. Dante, the medieval poet, saw Hell, Purgatory and Paradise arranged in concentric circles with God as the outer circle, the *primum mobile* or "prime mover." Similarly, in Christian theology, the circular nimbus surrounds the heads of saints and divine figures. The eternal circle combines with the cross, or the cross is contained within a circle. The ancient ruins at Stonehenge are arranged in a circle, indicating that the primitive peoples of Great Britain also sensed from somewhere deep within their beings the significance of the wholeness and unity represented therein. Most of the ancients, such as the Egyptians, Incas and Mayans, even conceived of time as a circle, as evidenced by their calendars. And when modern man builds his cities, he frequently, perhaps unconsciously, arranges them in circular patterns. Interestingly, there is also a theory in modern science that both time and space "bend"—may actually be circular.

The circle, of course, is only one of the various archetypal symbols of man. Others include the square, the cross, the triangle. the two-headed or two-faced god or idol, wings signifying the spiritual or creative force sensed in the universe, and others. Often, many of these symbols are combined to signify more than one idea of that which is intuitively sensed. In any case, to one who takes the time to study them and to see how they pervade the history, thought and expression of mankind throughout his various cultures, there can be little doubt that more than coincidence alone is responsible for their repeated recurrence. They are without a doubt the result of some deep, inner, collective experience. See the series of figures following.

The circle is the most common of all archetypal symbols. Over the ages, it has been interpreted as expressing in thousands of ways man's inherent craving for wholeness and his awareness of the universal, divine or creative forces at work in him and in the universe of which he is a part. The following might be so interpreted.

Figure 8-1.   Symbol from a very ancient Hindu table thousands of years old, showing the circle as God with rays emanating earthward to symbolize His creative action.

Figure 8-2.   This is a reproduction from an ancient stone table of almost the same era as Figure 8-1, but found in Mexico. This shows both the circle and representations of the four creative forces in the universe as perceived by early man—the "four great commands of creation, having to do with earth, air, fire and water. Ultimately these would find symbolization in the familiar cross of Christianity and all its variations.

Figure 8-3. The circle with the eye in the center, signifying the whole of creation. This symbol is found in almost all ancient cultures, and still
may be seen on American currency. For man still believes that the
creative force, the "eye of God," watches him.

Figure 8-4. This is another recurrent symbol throughout all human cultures—the
circle and the cross, signifying, again, man's archetypal perceptions
of the unity of creation and the sensed balance of its forces. This
symbol has been found in stone tablets from ancient civilizations as
divergent as Persia, Burma, Mexico and in the mythology of the
American Indian—not to mention its being a central symbol of
Christianity.

Following is another series of archetypal symbols that
illustrates the commonness and collectiveness of man's experience and his symbolic expression of that experience.
This is the winged circle, which combines in various ways
the ideas of the unity of the universe, the symmetry and
balance of the creative forces therein—almost invariably
four, usually referred to, depending on the culture, as the
"Four Great Builders," the "Heavenly Architects," the
"Great Primary Forces," the "Four Great Strong Ones," or
similar terminology.

Figure 8-5.   This is the Mexican "winged butterfly," the oldest known symbolic expression of the universe and its creative forces, dating back to 10,000 B.C.

Figure 8-6.   This is the oldest known refinement of the same idea, from an ancient Hindu manuscript. Here the wings signifying the "creative spirit" are feathered. Note also the cross within the circle. This symbol indicates another plateau in man's awakening consciousness and symbol-making capability.

Figure 8-7.   This figure is Guatemalan and shows another sophisticated, although very ancient, refinement of the same perception expressed on the other side of the earth by the Hindus.

Figure 8-8. This is an ancient Persian representation of the same archetypal idea. Here, a man has been added, signifying yet another step in the evolution of man's awareness of his relationship with the universe and its creative forces.

Figure 8-9. An ancient Assyrian representation of the winged circle.

Figure 8-10. The ancient Egyptians used the same winged circle quite extensively and in many variations. This example is from the tomb of Pharoah.

Figure 8-11. The Greeks, of course, were highly refined in this conceptualization of what they sensed within themselves to be the nature of the creation of which they were a part. They also were noted for their simplicity of design and the inherent profoundness of that simplicity. This winged circle is evidence of both.

Figure 8-12. The "thunderbird" of the American Indian, which has been adopted by a modern automobile manufacturer, somehow carrying through the original concept and association with power and force.

The foregoing illustrations represent only one of many possible sets of examples of how the internal, collectively unconscious perceptions of man have been expressed through his instinctive symbol-making capability throughout the ages. The significant point is that neither the original instinct nor the symbol-making capability is dead in modern man. As his artistic and verbal abilities have increased and become refined, he merely has become more elaborate and sophisticated in his expressions. By early

Christian times, he had already advanced well into his "verbal era." By medieval times, he was expressing the same basic urges in elaborate designs of his worshipping places, and today he still expresses them.

Figure 8-13. A medieval representation of Christ, showing the circular nimbus around his head—refining the original concept of the whole, divine, creative force, now becomes "God incarnate," or "God in man."

Figure 8-14. A highly elaborate, circular representation, or mandala, in a cathedral window.

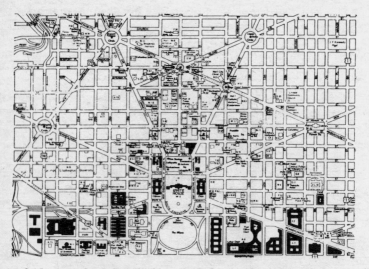

Figure 8-15. A modern city (Washington, D.C.) showing that modern man still instinctively cleaves to his original expressive urgings. Similar designs can be seen in other cities such as Paris and Rome.

Figure 8-16. The ancient ruins of Stonehenge, England, repeat the circular pattern.

Figure 8-17. A typical modern version of the original archetypal expression. Here is shown the shoulder patch of a twentieth century astronaut. Compare it with the earlier symbolic expression. The circle, the wholeness, are still present.

THE ARCHETYPAL DREAM

The archetypal dream, according to Jung and others, is an unconscious expression, similar to conscious symbol making, of some aspect of the history of man rolled up in each of us. It is the dream that emanates not from personal experience, but from the collective predispositions of mankind that each of us carries within. This type of dream occurs because, at the unconscious level, modern man preserves the same primitive symbol-making capability for expression of those Biblical "groanings that cannot be uttered."

The archetypal dream is not necessarily a frequent occurrence in the individual person. When it does occur, it may be passed over for the simple reason that the average person is not sufficiently familiar with the collective experience of mankind to relate and interpret the dream's symbology. The basic principle of understanding the context, as well as the contents, of a dream still applies. It is quite difficult to interpret such dreams without an extensive knowledge of such subjects as mythology, anthropology, and similar studies related to the historical development of man.

Regardless, the archetypal dream has a vital significance in the psychic existence of modern man. We respond in numerous ways to the ancient and archetypal capacities within us that originally found expression in religious ritual and symbol making. In times of national stress such as war or other conflict, these ingrained tendencies find expression in our collective behavior. They influence the moral temperament of the times. They tell of our collective fears and hopes. They account for some mass movements, for religious revivals, and for our regressions to the level of primitive violence. The full significance of archetypal dreams probably is not known, or known only to a few of the more insightful among us. That they do exist and have some purpose, however, may be definitely presumed— simply because anything that happens within the being of man has some purpose, whether it is understood at the moment or not. Perhaps the ultimate purpose of the archetypal dream is in fact to *express* that which cannot be expressed in any other way. Perhaps the archetypal dream is merely the voice of our ancestors reincorporated within us, their bones crying out to us, making known the deepest yearnings within each of us and the lessons that have been learned through the ages. Or, the archetypal dream could even be the voice of God Himself, if we choose to believe in God's existence.

Following is a dream Frank Foster had while attending Dr. Jung's Institute in Zurich, Switzerland:

> I was in a classroom with a raised platform for the teacher's desk. Behind the desk was a very old man who resembled Dr. Jung himself. He said directly to me, "Beware the degree Doctor of Crystals, it is useless."
>
> Zurich, 1964

There is a good chance that this dream was archetypal. It is apparent why the wise old man looked like Dr. Jung. He merely represented a very convenient image available to the unconscious. At this particular time in his life, the author had been quite deeply pondering and meditating upon the *real* goals of his ministerial life—essentially whether to proceed upon a scholarly, "preaching" pathway, which often can lead to a detachment from *real* involvement in ministering to the needs of people, or to "get out into the street and get involved."

Recall an earlier discussion of the greater reasoning and decision-making powers often available within the unconscious. These merge quite readily with the wise old man idea. It thus is quite logical, based upon a knowledge of the dreamer's larger life, to interpret this dream as essentially archetypal, while dealing with a current problem of the dreamer. The old man may well have represented an aspect of the dreamer's image of God Himself. The "degree of Doctor of Crystals"? Crystals are not true gems, although they deceptively sparkle as such. Could not the wise old man, perhaps the archetypal image of God in the dream, be warning that much academic study and preaching are not the true gems of the ministry, but merely the superficial "degree of Doctor of Crystals"? As the ancient writer of The Book of Ecclesiastes put it: "Of the making of many books there is no end; and much study is a weariness unto the flesh. Let us hear the end of the matter: Fear God, and keep his commandments: For this is the whole duty of the matter."

The above dream was one of a series. Following is another:

> I was fishing in a lake with an old man. I caught a brem in a sock or shoe. The old man is filling the lake with clear water. I ask if I can have the fish to eat and he says yes.
> Stuttgart, Germany, 1965

Again, the old man appears. This time, he and the dreamer were fishing. And the author was reminded of Jesus' words to Peter and Andrew, his first disciples, to "Follow me and I will make you fishers of men." The fish, of course, is highly significant as a symbol in the Christian faith and, because of the author's background, these associations must be taken into account. The fish is also a primary food source and, according to Edgar Cayce in his book on dreams, may represent "searching for spiritual food." The water, as already mentioned, is highly significant. It probably represents the depths which, at this time in his life, the dreamer was attempting to launch himself into or upon. The fact that the old man is giving clear water also is important—especially in the light of the first dream and the author's inner striving for clarity and direction in life.

Following are two more dreams that occurred at about the same time in the dreamer's life.

I was headed for my next destination. I was excited about it and began to run. Then I decided to try to leap and fly. I roared downstairs and fell at the bottom of the stairs. I was not hurt. I got up and there was fog in the valley. I walked through the fog with my uncle Scott McCane (recently deceased) to a beautiful seaside scene bathed in sunshine, clear and clean, and accented by ideal weather.

There we saw a wild female duck swimming on a quiet bay.

We went fishing.

Stuttgart, Germany, 1965

I dreamed of being in a building where there was construction going on—I went to a place on the second or third floor where there was a large archway with a curtain covering it. Outside were cards with students' names which were fastened to a bulletin board on the corner of the building. They were placed there by Dr.-------. One had my name on it with Latin and Greek inscriptions. The inscriptions had to do with teaching, possibly a Bible verse concerning one's aptness to teach.

Sara and I stood there together and discussed the possible significance of such inscriptions. Dr. Claus ------- came by and remarked that he was glad we found the card. I tried to engage him in conversation concerning the card but he excused himself as being in a hurry and left.

Stuttgart, Germany, 1965

As the reader will note, this series of dreams occurred several years ago. It was at a time of major decision making in the personal life of the dreamer. Much of the probable symbology in the last two dreams should be evident—the incident of fishing again, the reference to teaching (ministering), the stumbling while hurrying to get to a goal, again the old man or teacher, etc. Clearly, to Foster, these dreams bore a message of significance and meaning with respect to his life and mission in it.

Mambert has had similar dreams. Although we did not meet until several years later, at almost the same time that the above dreams were occurring in the life of one of us, the other was having dreams such as the following:

I was sleeping soundly. Suddenly, quite clearly and audibly, I heard the spoken words, "Get out of bed and get on your knees."

Falls Church, Virginia, 1965

Again, one must know something of the dreamer's overall life. Briefly, Mambert—on the other side of the Atlantic Ocean—also was undergoing a similar process of self examination and seeking of clarity in his life-calling. This particular dream is not as clearly identifiable as archetypal. Yet, we have found it of particular interest and relationship here, since we are fairly well-convinced that the crossing of our paths in life has been no mere accident. Any reader may make of this what he wishes. We shall see the further possible significance of these two sets of dreams as we discuss the concepts of the *superconscious* and *synchronicity*.

Mambert also has of times taken to setting his dreams down in poetic form. The following is an example.

The Face of God*

Good morning, God
I seek your face,
But instead—
I see
A black
Cherub
Boy, dressed spic and span,
Round faced,
Smiling,
Gleaming,
In boy scout
Uniform,
At proud,
Child attention.

What tricks
You play
Upon my
Mind—
God.

And now I see
An endless,
Shadow line
Beside him
To the right.

Down that
That
Haunting,
Seeming
Endless line.

---

*From *Sadhappy and Other Thoughts By WAM*, Communication Institute. 1973.

My eyes
Search to see
Your face,
God

Along
The ghostly,
Faceless,
Indian multitude
I scan.

A shriveled,
Shrouded,
Cobwebbed,
Aged man
I see.
His toothless
Face
And bony arm.

A ballerina
Child
I see.
She whirls
And pirouettes
In pink,
And smiles,
Bright,
With
Sparkling eye
And
Tender
Little
Feet.
A nursing mother,
Now I see.
With baby at her breast.

But still
Along
This
Single,
Infinite

Cordon,
No face of God
I see.

And so I search,
And seek,
And peer
Along this
Gray,
Enshrouded,
Endless line.

The reader should be able to see the relationship of the ideas in this dream-poem to some of the ideas in Foster's dreams. There are several possible archetypal expressions here; for example, the child, the nursing mother, and of course the old man. What is the dream saying? For the dreamer it said: "This is your answer to where you might find the face of God for which you have been searching. It is in reality the faces of all these people. One cannot help but be reminded here of the following New Testament passage:

> You have my Father's blessing; come, enter and possess the kingdom that has been ready for you since the world was made. For when I was hungry you gave me food; when thirsty, you gave me drink, when I was a stranger, you took me into your home, when naked you clothed me; when I was ill you came to my help, when in prison you visited me. Then the righteous will reply, "Lord, when was it that we saw you hungry and fed you, or thirsty and gave you drink, a stranger and took you home, or naked and clothed you? When did we see you ill or in prison and once to visit you?" And the king will answer, "I tell you this: anything that you did for one of my brothers here, however humble, you did for me."

We realize that all readers may not share our belief in the synchronicity of things. Therefore, we again merely suggest that each reader make of these allusions what he wishes.

RECOGNIZING THE ARCHETYPAL DREAM

The same basic rules of all dream interpretation apply here, although identification of the dream material and its interpretation are more difficult. The best initial approach is to be ready and open to the possibility, and then to establish the knowledge base that will make identification possible. A knowledge of history and mythology is almost an absolute necessity. At best, the layman may be able to merely identify the *possibility* that he has had an archetypal dream. Yet, if the interest is present, he may also be able to obtain its interpretation through additional study and research. Following is a suggested procedure for determining whether or not you may have had an archetypal dream and for beginning to find an interpretation for it.

1. Naturally, make as complete and accurate a written record of the dream as you possibly can, as soon after awakening as possible.
2. Take particular note of any visual images, especially arrangements of objects and people into identifiable patterns.
3. Take particular note of whether or not you can relate an occurrence or image to something in your personal life, something that you can personally remember or account for in your own experience. A frequent characteristic of the archetypal dream is the fact that it usually cannot be related to the personal experience of the dreamer.
4. Take particular note of any "voice," "light," "essence," or "presence," that seems to be coming from somewhere "outside" of the setting of your dream itself.
5. Make drawings of any patterns, objects, or symbols that you experience as soon after awakening as possible.

6. Take particular note of anything that seems to have a universal significance, as opposed to a personal relationship. A dream containing a panoramic view of the heavens would be an example. A dream of some ritual, perhaps religious, or even of witchcraft, would be another example. This does not mean that you believe in witchcraft. Much of the symbolism connected with that practice, however, arises from the deep archetypal fears and conflicts within man with respect to such subjects as "heaven and hell," "good and evil," "positive and negative," etc. Another obvious example, of course, would be an out-and-out dream of God or of the Devil. These too are representations of very *archaic* vestiges within your being. Some other examples would include:

Dreams of heroes, such as knights, redeemers, rescuers, etc.

Dreams of sacrifices, initiation, fertility rites and similar ritualistic occurrences

"Visions" of religious figures, divinities or activities

Dreams of chases, hunts, sexuality, etc.

Dreams containing images that might be interpreted as representing universal womanhood or manhood

Dreams of great masses of people, parades, huge battles, or prehistoric animals

Dreams of fire, earth, vast expanses of water, violent storms, being chased by wild animals, or partly human beasts

The reason for taking note of such as these is that they are often representative of very fundamental and recurring human experiences. They may not always be archetypal, but the chances of their being so are greater than with simple, more-or-less everyday imagery, events, people or figures.

7. Finally, once you have noted and recorded the material in your dream, you must research and compare it with the various available historical sources.

The foregoing is admittedly a very brief summary of how man's collective, archetypal imperatives or instincts express themselves in his conscious and unconscious worlds. It obviously would be possible to write several volumes on this aspect of the unconscious alone, which Dr. Jung has already done. This, however, should serve to illustrate the point that there is strong indication that there is such a thing as the collective unconscious—or at least a collective experience—which manifests itself in the conscious expressions of man. This same collective experience is recorded somewhere within each individual person, and also naturally manifests itself in his personal, unconscious experience, particularly in his dreams. It also is quite likely to relate to an individual's current problems, and most definitely relates to the quest for personal wholeness.

SUMMARY

We again emphasize that the archetype is *not the idea itself*, but the universal experience, awareness or predisposition to produce the idea or a symbol representing it.

Undoubtedly, the interpretation and understanding of any archetypal dreams that you may have, or suspect that you may have, will be among the most difficult of your interpretive work. Yet, the discoveries that you may make also can be the most revelatory and rewarding kind. For it is through this process that you may come to, among other things, a deeper and fuller understanding of your true relationship with and connection to all of mankind. You can attain a new sense of wholeness and greater awareness of the fact that you are not completely alone in the universe. You also will come to a fuller understanding of yourself and how you fit into the scheme of things. You will become a wiser person, for you will have tapped the "wisdom of the ages." In no small or meaningless way, in fact, your archetypal dream could be the "voice" of God Himself speaking to you.

9
The
Superconscious

Most modern psychiatrists limit their division of the human mind to the categories of the conscious and the unconscious (sometimes the subconscious). Yet, a total perspective demands a look at some capabilities and activities of the mind that do not readily fit into these categories. Some things cannot be explained solely in terms of the personal conscious or unconscious, or even the collective unconscious. We speak here of those mental activities, manifestations and phenomena usually grouped under the heading of *parapsychology* or *spiritualism*. Parapsychology means literally "like psychology but not psychology." This is really a misnomer. For *anything* that pertains to the *psyche*, real or imagined, simply because it is of or does relate to the psyche, rightfully comes under the heading of psychology. Just because something is unexplained or unsubstantiated does not mean that it does not belong to the field in which it happens. Following are the main examples of the types of mental activities, manifestations, phenomena, or ideas about these things, that usually fall within this nomenclature:

1. God, as an idea or a phenomenon
2. The human soul, as an idea or a phenomenon
3. Spiritual, as opposed to physical, law or principle
4. Synchronicity—meaningful coincidence, "fate," "destiny," or the existence of some connecting purpose in events
5. Positive-negative psychic energy or force, for example, personal proneness to certain types of occurrences such as accidents or success
6. Communication with the dead or spirits, such as that presumably experienced by psychic mediums
7. Spiritual manifestations such as "ghosts," poltergeists or doppelgangers
8. Visions and revelations such as those experienced by Biblical characters or people who claim to have seen the Virgin Mary
9. Astralprojection—leaving one's body
10. Mental telepathy (mindreading)—direct mental contact between people without spoken words
11. Clairvoyance—discerning objects or events not present to the senses
12. Extrasensory perception (ESP)—knowing or experiencing (particularly the future) without the physical senses
13. Telekinesis—control of physical objects without touching them, through mental power alone
14. Teleportation—projection or movement of self by mental power
15. Precognition—knowing or seeing the future
16. Prayer and healing

Another term that has recently come into use to identify the realm within which mental, emotional or spiritual activities such as the above occur is the *superconscious*. Edgar Cayce, the psychic researcher, described the superconscious as that portion of man's mind which has retained its knowledge of God's presence. One can see the connection here with the idea of the collective unconscious, and particularly the God imperative, as described earlier. Others are more content with such descriptions as "the spiritual realm," "parapsychology," the "supernatural," or even the "twilight zone." It really does not matter how one labels what is observed. The fact remains that certain things do happen, absurd or logical, and that they cannot be fully explained in terms of the generally accepted categories. The main purpose of this chapter is to group these occurrences in a way that is convenient for their examination as a part of the total psychic activity of human beings. For it is clear that they cannot be ignored by anyone seeking a full understanding of his own psyche.

THE PROBLEMS OF SCIENCE

Science in its present state of development has some problems with the idea of the superconscious. One of the reasons for this relates to the twentieth century tendency for the scientist to overreact to those things generally considered to be occult or supernatural in medieval terms. "Occult" really means nothing more than "that which is hidden or unknown." It would seem that the scientist would be anxious to penetrate the unknown. But this may not be the case; he may arbitrarily decide which *part* of the unknown he wishes to penetrate and ignore the rest of it.

Another reason for the lag in scientific examination of the realm of the superconscious is that it does not seem to yield as easily as the physical sciences do to scientific methods of data gathering and observation. Most physical phenomena occur and may be observed on an objective basis and measured under controlled conditions external to the bias of the researcher or observer. If a scientist wishes to conduct an experiment, it is relatively easy for him to set up the necessary controlled conditions. As physical data are gathered and observed, they usually exhibit consistencies, and hence a predictability evolves. From that predictability, a "natural law" in turn evolves, and more frequently than not, even its exceptions will be consistent and predictable. So far, this has not been the case in the realm of the superconscious.

Comparing the basic science of psychology itself to the physcial sciences—without regard for its upper range of parapsychology—one becomes almost immediately aware that the same kind of objectivity and evolution of "laws" and "principles" are much more difficult to come by. The problems of subjectivity and variability in many cases seem almost insurmountable. Moving into the realm of the parapsychological or superconscious, the problems of subjectivity, variability and unpredictability become even more pronounced and intensified. Science in its present form seems unable to cope with them. Only the most daring scientist is likely to come out and say that he is exploring the field, and then at the risk of the ridicule and disdain of other members of his profession.

The most intelligent and realistic position, it would seem, is to take psychic events—whatever their source or cause, however absurd or ridiculous they seem to be—as raw data for examination and the possible drawing of some hypothesis from them. Cautious openness and receptivity seem far the better reaction than slamming the door simply because we do not have a crucible in which to contain that which is observed. An hypothesis is already indicated: There is *something* present and occurring that so far appears to be at least a partial extension beyond what we normally consider to be the conscious and unconscious powers of the human mind. This is the position the authors hold.

THE SUPERCONSCIOUS IN HISTORY

It is quite well accepted that history often lends important clues to that which is being observed in the present day. This undoubtedly has something to do with earlier man's apparent greater intouchness with his total self. Although he frequently articulated this intouchness in terms that are now unacceptable to modern man (demons, witches, etc.), it is uncanny how he so often closely approximated the later, "scientific" discovery and articulation. The history and literature of mankind are replete with references to and records of presumed manifestations of what we call the superconscious, as both a concept and a phenomenon. The pervasiveness of the recordings alone are staggering. This, in fact, is probably the best-documented observation throughout the history of man. Among all races and cultures, ideas such as man's having a soul, the existence of some kind of spirit world, communication with the dead, and of course the existence of God, are present. The average reader probably isn't fully aware of just how much must be refuted in order to deny the existence of the superconscious or its equivalent. Almost all of the writers of classical times—Socrates, Plato, Herodotus, Sophocles, Euripides, Aristotle, Horace, Cicero, Virgil, Homer, Plutarch, Josephus, to mention but a few—repeatedly referred to the existence of this realm. The entire cosmology of the world is founded upon it. For Christian, Jew, Moslem, Hindu, Confucianist and Buddhist alike, to negate the superconscious is to reject and remove the underpinnings and foundations of their whole faiths. The Bible, the writings of the Apostolic Fathers, of the founders of all Protestant religions (Wesley, Knox, Luther, Calvin, etc.), all lose their fundamental premises; their logic disintegrates. Further, numerous revered scholars, presidents, leaders, philosophers, etc., become little more than deluded mumblers. Psychologists such as Jung and modern theologians such as Swedenborg, Kierkegaard, Maritain, Buber, Tillich, Barth, etc., all become suspect in their reasoning. The existence of the "other," transpersonal side of man thus seems irrefutable. The modern view of those who believe that there is something at least worth investigating is perhaps best summed up in the words of the Reverend Doctor George M. Searle, Rector of the Church of Saint Paul the Apostle, New York City, who said that the reality of the spiritual world is not even open to question any more. Anyone who doesn't know this is simply not up to date. "I do not believe in spirits," said Swedenborg, "I have seen too many of them."

THE RELATION TO THE COLLECTIVE UNCONSCIOUS

There seems little doubt that what we call the superconscious may be closely related and connected to the collective unconscious, as described earlier. It could, in fact, be considered as merely an extension of the unconscious although this would still leave some things unexplained. The idea of God or of apparent spiritual manifestations external to the individual person would require further elucidation. The best example of their connection, however, is the comparison of the superconscious to man's retention of some memory of the presence of God. This, too, is a believable explanation for such legendary and mythological stories as the Biblical Garden of Eden—perhaps merely man's archetypal memory of the force that created him. One sees the same sort of thing repeated in microcosm in the individual human being. The Chinese, in fact, have taken the position that man is a duplicated microcosm of the larger universe. As a child, each of us begins life with an undifferentiated, nascent sense of wholeness, and only after the fragmenting, *dis*integrating effects of living collectively in society begin to break down this archetypal wholeness, do we begin to lose touch with the various parts of our beings—including our superconscious. Perhaps the Biblical "a little child shall lead them," or Jesus' admonition that "Unless ye become as little children, ye shall not see the kingdom of heaven," are more profound than many of us might suspect. What, after all, could "heaven" be besides unity, harmony, attunement with the Infinite, as well as inner personal adjustment in the present life. Perhaps this too is why Jesus said "nor will they say, 'Lo here it is!' or 'There!' the kingdom of God is within you" (or, "in the midst of you").

In any case, no one can be quite sure as to exactly where the archetypal "memory" leaves off and the so-called superconscious takes up within the psyche of man. This shouldn't be too difficult to live with if one stops to remember that wholeness and interrelationship are the keys to understanding, and the ultimate goal. The simple fact is that all parts are intimately related and flow into and with each other. What we call the superconscious thus appears to be a flowing and permeating energy or force coexistent with the rest of man's psychic makeup, possibly extending beyond or outside his inner self into some attunement or connection with the larger universe. Or, for that matter, it could be that the superconscious is representative of the "whole that is greater than the sum of its parts."

DREAMS AND THE SUPERCONSCIOUS

We have already shown how the dream state is very conducive to the tapping of greater reserves within the unconscious. There is also considerable evidence that the superconscious behaves in a similar way. For some reason, not yet fully understood, there seems to be a greater tendency for occurrences such as those listed to take place when the mind is in a dream or dream-like state. The primary reason for this probably is because the whole mind is freer and less occupied in the dream state than in the conscious state. One must, of course, be very careful in associating his dreams with activities of the superconscious. The soundest approach always will be to seek first the association in terms of *intra*personal conscious or unconscious activities, exhausting all possibilities, in order to be sure that only genuine *extra*personal experiences and occurrences are attributed to the superconscious.

Some of the best examples of dreams which might be attributed to the superconscious and its connection with some external force or energy source are found in the Bible. The best known of these are in connection with the birth of Jesus:

> The angel of the Lord appeared unto him [Joseph, the father of Jesus] in a dream, saying, "Joseph, thou son of David, fear not to take unto thee Mary for thy wife: for that which is conceived in her is of the Holy Ghost. And she shall bring forth a son, and thou shalt call his name Jesus: for he shall save his people from their sins.
>
> *Matthew 2:13*

Joseph was also purportedly warned in a dream of King Herod's intent to kill the child Jesus and to flee into Egypt. After the death of Herod, he was told in a dream to return to Israel. The story of the shepherds and their purported sightings of messengers from God also would be classifiable as an activity of the superconscious in relation to some external or transpersonal force. Another famous Biblical dream or dreamlike experience interpretable as a manifestation of some form of superconscious activity is the Book of the Apocalypse, or Revelation, presumably written by a man named John. (Perhaps this man was the Apostle John who wrote that he had personally seen both the miracles of Christ and his definitely transpersonal ascension.)

> I was in the Spirit [apparently a trance, or dreamlike state] on the Lord's day, and heard a great voice as of a trumpet, saying I am Alpha and Omega, the first and the last: and what thou seest write in a book . . .

Following this passage comes some of the loftiest and most profound literature ever written, replete with symbology, having to do with both the past and the future of mankind. Modern theologians still base much of their thought and religious practice on this ancient dream—which unequivocally claims to be a direct communication from God!

One of the best-known events of a similar nature in modern times is that of Joseph Smith, founder of the Mormon Church. Smith claimed to have been visited by an angel named Moroni and that the entire Book of Mormon, as well as his instructions to lead his people to Great Salt Lake, Utah, came to him as direct revelation from God. Considering the success of the project, it is quite difficult to gainsay the possibility that there was some form of extrapersonal guidance involved. Ventures such as this usually need "a little something extra," no matter where it might come from. Even if only extreme personal motivation were the source of the energy needed, this alone would seem to transcend the mundane powers of the mind.

Edgar Cayce, who died in 1945, kept what is probably one of the most thoroughly documented records of activity attributable to the superconscious. In the files of the Association for Research and Enlightenment, with national headquarters at Virginia Beach, Virginia, there are records of over 14,246 psychic occurrences, involving thousands of people, as recorded by Cayce during his lifetime. Of these, 1,009 are dream interpretations, many being provable substantiations of extrapersonal experience. Numerous cases, as yet to be cataloged, are on file in the archives of almost every major newspaper in the world. One such case was reported in the *Houston Post* of February 18, 1964. During the night of February 17 of that year, as he sat reading, an Air Force Master Sergeant named James Lee, living in Wichita Falls, received a telephone call from his mother-in-law in Clovis, New Mexico, some three hundred miles away. She told him she had just dreamed that something terrible had happened to her daughter. So far as he knew, Lee's wife was alive and well, sleeping in another room. He went to her room and found her dead. Another famous case reported by Cayce concerns the 1966 landslide tragedy in the Welsh town of Aberfan where a huge coal-slag heap came down a mountainside and killed one hundred and forty-four people. A Dr. J. C. Baker, M.D., of Shropshire, England, compiled a list of thirty townspeople who swore that they had dreamed of the disaster before it occurred. There are thousands of cases similar to these on record, many of which are apparently substantiated by witnesses from all walks of life.

THE PRECOGNITIVE DREAM

The genuinely *precognitive* dream differs from the personally *predictive* dream as described earlier. The former means to *know*; the latter means to assume a probability that something will happen. The predictive dream remains basically an internal personal experience. That is, the inner reasoning processes of the dreamer in reality are merely projecting ahead of his conscious thinking and actions and carrying a given course of events to its logical conclusion. This type of dream merely tells the dreamer what *can* happen if certain things that he is doing, thinking or experiencing continue in a certain way without alteration. It is, in effect, a warning to him that his conscious should intervene. The precognitive dream, however, foretells a specific happening irrespective of such an extrapolation, or of personal action. Prior to the assassination of John F. Kennedy, for example, numerous people (as reported later) had dreamed either of the forthcoming tragedy or at least that "something bad" was going to happen to him. Even in some of these dreams, a good case could be made for the possibility that Kennedy may have been a shadow figure for some of the dreamers. And, had Kennedy himself dreamed of his assassination, the dream could have been interpreted as predictive and not precognitive, since he was probably both consciously and unconsciously aware that he had set up the conditions, was on a course of action, that *could* lead to his assassination. Nevertheless, in some cases the pre-knowing of the event could be interpreted as a genuine superconscious view of the future.

Frequently, a precognitive dream will not be recognizable as such until after the pre-known event occurs. This is especially true if the symbology of the dream is obscure, or if there is no apparent association within the present conscious life of the dreamer. For example, one young woman in California had a recurrent dream that there were snakes in her backyard. The dream had no particular meaning until a forest fire occurred in the area. In her yard one day, she actually stepped on a baby rattler. Many snakes had been driven into the residential area by the fire.

The best way to be sure as to whether or not a dream is precognitive or clairvoyant is alertness, careful observation and record keeping. Many people undoubtedly have had precognitive dreams without being aware that they have had them. This sometimes accounts for the feeling of "having been here before" that many people experience. Keeping a careful dream diary will help immeasurably in this.

GOD AND THE NUMINOUS EXPERIENCE

We have already seen that the idea of God, or the God imperative, is in all probability archetypal or inherent in man. That is, speaking solely from the internal human standpoint, without regard for any supernatural aspects, God exists for man. But to literally billions of human beings over the centuries, God has been far more than a mere impulse or instinct within man himself. He has been an external force as well. Here again, "He" exists even if "He" is nothing more than the composite of observable attributes, purposes, natural laws and evidences of unity and harmony obviously present in the universe and creation. All of these things are known to exist. They therefore exist no matter what man calls them. If he chooses to call them "God," God exists. The reasoning, however, must advance yet another step further. For, in the words of the New Testament writer of the Book of Hebrews, "we are also compassed about by a great cloud of witnesses" of yet another sort. We speak here of the great multitude of human beings, both past and present, who have testified (many on pain of death) that they have *personally experienced* God as more than and in addition to any of the above. That is, you have actually the greater bulk of humanity who, were they required to stand in a court of law and give testimony by the standards that prove or disprove, would testify to experiencing God in some way as a *communicative personality*. One is staggered to think of the actual size of this multitude of witnesses, not to mention the range of their intelligences and reasoning capabilities.

The word "numinous" derives from a Latin term meaning "spirit," or more accurately "divine force or spirit." The numinous experience, therefore, is any personal experience attributable to an interaction of man with God. It relates both to the God imperative that exists within man and to God as an external, personal force. Here again, one must not limit oneself by thinking in terms that are too narrow. For the spiritual experience may take many forms.

It could well take the form of that which is explainable in rational and scientific terms. But it also may take the form of that which is irrational, totally outside any known way of reasoning or considering things. The best and most widespread example of this numinous experience is the so-called "conversion experience." This is especially evident in, although not limited to, the Christian religion. For some reason not fully (although perhaps partially) explainable in the generally accepted psychological terminology, people still have "confrontations with God," or perhaps more accurately, confrontations with *themselves* and God. A part of this experience often seems to be external to the person himself, and hence we relate it to the idea of the super-conscious.

Dreams afford one of the most convenient sources for examining the nature of the numinous experience, chiefly because the human psyche is most "ready" for the experience when it is in this state. The reason for this should be fairly easy to see. Dreaming not only places a person in greater touch with the fuller resources and capabilities of his mind, it also returns a person to the most fundamental "connections" that exist within, between and among the various parts of his psyche—the personal unconscious, the collective unconscious and the superconscious. In other words, it links him with his *total being* in a way in which he cannot be connected while in the relatively limited conscious state. There are some exceptions to this, for example, in certain meditative states and maybe even under some hallucinatory conditions.

Reason and the rational actually become the limiting and restricting factors in experiencing the numinous. Jung calls reason the "greatest and most tragic illusion" of man. Reason actually is far more subjective than its tenets claim. For example, it claims that all phenomena must be considered and explained in its (reason's) own terms. What could be more unreasonable? The inherent fallacy here is self-evident. One reason that Jung and others sometimes called the collective unconscious the *objective* unconscious is that it indeed does contain objective data, unrestricted by subjective reason, irrespective of the opinions of man. In it, things merely occur, explainable, rational or irrational. So it is with at least a part of the superconscious.

One should be able to see here the connection with the idea of the truly individuated, whole person—who cannot be truly whole without the whole experience of which he is capable—which includes the numinous experience! The practical answer for the individual person seeking security within himself (and this is the secret yearning of every one of us) should be obvious. It is clear that reason alone fails to provide us with this security. Even the reasoned theology fails us. The rationalists insist that if everybody were "logical and reasonable," all human problems would be solvable. This simply is not true. For each of us still would be out of touch with his whole self. Reason makes motors run, often cures physical illnesses and brings social peace, but it is relatively powerless to bring inner peace or cure the soul. These must come from within the psyche—the soul itself—from a numinous conversation with God, in terms of whatever understanding one has of Him.

It is tragically interesting that even organized religion—which, when one stops to think about it, has become largely based upon systems of logic—actually propels man away from and not (as presumed) toward a direct numinous experiencing of God. The Bible, the creed, the catechism, the doctrine, the ritual, are often barriers instead of bridges between the mind of man and God. Religionists today often ask why God does not so often speak directly to man as he is reported to have done in former times. One rabbi has answered this: "Nowadays there is nobody who can bow low enough." In other words, there are few who can get themselves into the attuned, "intouch" state—or to listen when they are in such a state—for example, while dreaming. The Catholic Church carries in its official creed the idea of *somnia a Deo missa* (dreams sent by God). The Protestant minister and the rabbi preach of the dreams of Daniel, Joseph, Pharoah, the Virgin Mary, etc. But were a present day parishioner or communicant in any faith to come to the priest, minister or rabbi with a report of hearing the *Vox Dei* (voice of God) in a dream, he would most likely be told that "reason must prevail." Many ministers have told the authors that they consider dreams to be little more than nonsense; hence, by their own admission, their own Bible is nonsense.

What conclusion can be drawn for the reader of this book? It is simply this: If intelligence and reason must prevail, is it not more reasonable and intelligent to remain open and listening for the voice of God, or for any other voice, than to shut up the eyes and ears and not even allow that there might be voices to hear?

THE "HOLY SPIRIT"

If there is such a thing as the human superconscious, it supports the concept of what the Christian calls the Holy Spirit and which other religions also refer to as the Tao, the Divine Creative Force, the Earthly Power of God, etc. Jesus told his disciples that he would not "leave them comfortless," but would send them a "comforter" who, among other things, would "bring all things to their remembrance" that they needed to know in order to propagate the faith that he established. Also known as the Holy Ghost, this mysterious creative power is a central concept in every branch of the Christian religion. The more mundane interpreters of human behavior and belief refer to this essence as perhaps nothing more than the "conscience of man." But there appears to be more to it than this. The religionist sees the Holy Spirit as the earthly Presence of God. To the Christian, the Holy Spirit is clearly the possessing and inspiring of men by God; the force behind wisdom, leadership, conversion, judgment, moral character, prophesying, etc. To the scientific researcher, He must be considered as existing for all of the same reasons that God also must be considered as existing. In many respects, one might, in fact, merely capitalize the word Superconscious and use it interchangeably with the term Holy Spirit.

SPIRITUAL LAW

The idea of the superconscious also includes what is commonly referred to as *spiritual law*. This has to do with the supposition that there are certain natural laws in the spiritual or psychic realm similar to those that have been discovered in the physical universe. These are not laws in the legislative or physical sense, of course. They are in reality observable and predictable consistencies and are merely thought of as "laws" in the sense that they can be used to predict and describe the observable in nature. For example, it has been observed that a body will continue in a state of rest or motion unless acted upon by an external force. This phenomenon has been codified as Newton's first law of motion. Another observable phenomenon is that a mass, M, acted upon by an unbalanced force, F, will experience an acceleration a. Thus, $F = Ma$ which has been cataloged under the title of Newton's second law of motion. The observable fact that every physical force generates an equal and opposite force and the "law" of gravity are other examples of physical phenomena which have been quantified by the scientist in such a manner that they can be used to predict other observables. These laws can, for example, be used to predict that all objects regardless of size, shape or weight fall at the same rate in a vacuum. These same laws can also be used to correctly predict that the period of a pendulum is proportional to the square root of the length of the pendulum divided by the acceleration due to gravity ($T = 2\pi\sqrt{\frac{I}{G}}$). Each of these physical laws is a "law" only because it *correctly* describes natural phenomena. When exceptions are found, the laws are discarded or modified to account for the new observations. The laws do not control nature—they merely describe it!

Few people have difficulty in understanding and accepting the existence and validity of these laws once they are understood and demonstrated. Turning to the intangible or spiritual realm, however, one encounters the familiar difficulties of observation and discovering predictable consistencies. For, apparently, whatever spiritual laws are, they do not operate or manifest themselves in a way that man has yet been able to observe and record in order to satisfactorily prove their presence to all observers. But the physical laws, too, were mysteries until someone unravelled their mechanics. Some of them, such as $E = MC^2$ (Einstein's theory of relativity) were in fact *theories* before they became laws. So it seems to be with spiritual law. Some people are more convinced than others. The best that most current thinkers can seem to agree on is the most fundamental hypothesis that there is such a thing as spiritual law. We could be wrong, but the evidence is mounting to support this hypothesis that there are some principles in the spiritual realm that parallel those in the physical.

One example of what is meant by spiritual law, and perhaps the most provable one to date, is what the authors call "the law of faith." That is, there seems to be a very strong connection, insofar as psychic activity is concerned, between what a person believes will happen and what does happen. For example, there are very few cases on record of people who have not believed in God having any direct experience with Him. There are some cases, but very few. The same applies to most of the other psychic phenomena listed at the beginning of this chapter. There thus may well be a spiritual law of some kind involved.

A more down-to-earth example of what we mean by spiritual law can be seen in what the authors and other investigators have come to call the "law of proneness." Psychologists have long suspected that it is possible for a person to "set himself up" for either positive or negative events, misfortune or good fortune, by establishing what might be called a "psychological aura" or predisposition around himself. The most common example of this is "accident proneness."

Another common idea that fits at least partially into the idea of spiritual law is what psychologists call "psychosomatic illness." This may, in fact, be the best-documented area. For, it has almost definitely been established by many medical authorities that numerous physical ailments are direct results of disruptions in the inner mental, emotional or spiritual harmony of the ill person.

Philosophy and religion, of course, have always been replete with statements of spiritual laws. Can anyone doubt, for example, that Shakespeare's "This above all, to thine own self be true, and it must follow as night the day, thou canst not then be false to any man" is not an almost immutable truism. "Unless a man is born again, he shall not see the kingdom of heaven," as stated in the Gospel of John, is another. Following are some more examples of this type of spiritual law, from among the thousands that have been recorded:

> As a man thinketh in his heart, so is he. *(Proverbs 23:7)*
>
> People seldom improve when they have no model other than themselves to copy after. (Oliver Goldsmith)
>
> Trust in God, but keep your powder dry. (Oliver Cromwell)
>
> The best lightning rod for your protection is your own spine. (Ralph Waldo Emerson)

Self-reliance and self-respect are about as valuable commodities as we can carry in our pack through life. (Luther Burbank)

God helps those who help themselves. (Anonymous)

Liberty cannot exist without virtue. (Jean Jacques Rousseau)

Love gives itself; it is not bought. (Henry Wadsworth Longfellow)

We are shaped and fashioned by what we love. (Johann Wolfgang von Goethe)

SYNCHRONICITY

An example of another phenomenon which may have some connection within the idea of the superconscious is what Jung called *synchronicity*, or meaningful coincidence. The significance here lies in the word "meaningful." Some people also call this phenomenon "fate" or "destiny." There are many coincidences in life, unrelated and not caused by each other. Some have no meaning whatsoever. But there also are many coincidences still uncaused by each other (so far as is known or observable), but nevertheless when observed together seem to have *meaning*. Take for example, the case of a young woman of our acquaintance. On a certain day, for no apparent reason, she was seized with an almost uncontrollable urge to visit her mother in a neighboring city. When she awoke that morning, she had no intention of going to see her mother. But as the day wore on she decided that she would definitely make the visit that evening and spend the night. Had she stayed at her own apartment that night, she would have been killed or seriously injured when a part of the ceiling directly above her bed gave way and showered some fifty pounds of plaster and masonry upon the exact spot where her head normally would have been. These two events, the visit and the collapsing ceiling, obviously could not have had any causal relationship. But they did have an after-the-fact *meaningful* relationship; they had synchronicity. Numerous such synchronistic events occur in the lives of people every day. No one knows exactly why. Some researchers surmise that they may involve some form of unaware clairvoyance or ESP. Others think that some of them might have a sort of spontaneous source in the unconscious, interacting perhaps with external "vibrations." In any case they seem to be transpersonal and to involve some form of mental or psychic activity, either internal or external, of the persons who experience them. They would certainly seem to be at least partially includable under our investigative category of the superconscious.

Again, much of the problem that people experience in accepting the possibility of some kind of synchronicity, spiritual law, etc., lies in the basic inability to see what the breadth of such things might include. Whatever it is, it is in all probability just as "natural" as physical law is. And like most of the physical laws, it probably is right before our eyes waiting to be discovered by those who are looking for it. The basis is already present. That is based upon what is already known about the order, structure, logic and purpose of our being, it is more logical to assume some sort of purpose, meaning or cause in the extrapersonal psychic events that take place in our environment. What we thus have is a working hypothesis. And we must, of course, be ready to alter or abandon it if the hard evidence so indicates.

SIN, SATAN AND NEGATIVISM

This is what we might call the other side of the coin of spiritual law. The Bible says, "To him that knoweth to do good and doeth it not; to him this is sin." Webster's New International Dictionary defines sin as "to violate divine law." The average modern thinker tends to have the same kind of rational hangups with ideas like sin and Satan that he has with some of the other traditional, anthropomorphic statements of fundamental spiritual or moral truths. To many people, sin is the violation of a specific "rule" or admonition listed in some creed or catechism. And Satan is an actual person, perhaps with cloven hooves, et al. Interestingly, this concept of Satan is not even "according to scripture." For the Bible describes him as a "creature of light and tempting beauty"—which seems somewhat more in keeping with the presumed enticements that he offers to men.

We cannot rule out the possibility that Satan is an actual personality, for we do not know. Nor does anyone else. We think it is more likely, however, that this anthropomorphism, in the light of present knowledge, is too limiting—just as the idea of God as an old man with a long white beard is too restrictive. What one probably is dealing with is a force or energy, partially within and partially outside of man—a negative energy source undoubtedly very similar to the proneness idea just described. The reality is likely closer to the description given by St. Paul that "we wrestle with powers and principalities." That is, there can be little doubt that there is disharmony and negativism in the human situation. If there is such a thing as spiritual law, which there seems to be even if that law is nothing more than the natural harmony, functionalism and the unity of things, there would presumably have to be its opposite—which in effect would be the "breaking" of spiritual law.

Take, for example, the type of day or period in life, which almost all of us have experienced, when "nothing seems to go right." Many psychologists have observed how both the positive and the negative forces seem to "cluster," or to group themselves around given people at given times. For example, one gets up out of bed on a certain day, perhaps angry, irritable and feeling negative to begin with.

This may well be the result of some activity of the unconscious, collective unconscious or superconscious in the dreaming state, even if it is not remembered. (Recall that all of these have an influence upon waking activity and behavior, often consciously unknown to the person himself.) It then becomes an "off-on-the-wrong-foot" sort of day. A button drops off of a garment, the morning toast is burned, a finger is cut. Perhaps the shower water will not adjust properly. An argument may begin almost spontaneously with another member of the family. The mood increases and becomes intensified. On the way to work a near-accident occurs, and throughout the day events accumulate to make it a totally negative day.

The same sort of thing can happen on a broader life scale. One young man we know seems to have nothing but bad luck. He has failed in three attempts to start a business, been divorced twice, has had two children born with handicaps, and generally has every reason to indeed think that some "devil" or negative spirit is accompanying him throughout life. He naturally has developed a very pessimistic attitude toward life and people in general. He *expects* the worst to happen, and it usually does.

Some psychologists would completely rationalize that such a person has indeed "set himself up with a negative aura" or a "proneness" that will continue to attract like-happenings very similarly to the way that like-molecules in physical matter display the propensity to adhere to each other. The similarity here to Newton's law of inertia is remarkable; that a body moving in a certain direction will do so until intercepted by a greater force. It usually does take some kind of major regenerative experience in the life of such a person in order to alter the established course of his life; perhaps even being "born again" as Jesus put it to Nicodemus in the third chapter of the Gospel of John.

Consider here also what has been said earlier about the

predictive type of dream which tells the dreamer that if a given course of events continues without some conscious intervening action on the part of the dreamer, certain things will have a high probability of happening. With such thinking, the connections become almost immediately apparent, the forces and energies at work in this realm of the superconscious thrust themselves undeniably upon one.

Remember we are not saying here that there definitely are any transpersonal or extrapersonal negative forces (or positive), nor are we unequivocally attributing them to any external personality. What we are saying is that there *seems* to be at least some negative aspect such as this involved. This force also gives considerable indication of being at least partially extrapersonal, although also partially controllable at the personal level. In any case, these characteristics fit easily into the concept of the superconscious.

PRAYER AND HEALING

One consistently hears firsthand reports of the power of prayer in healing and rectifying both the physical and spiritual ills of men and women. Many readers themselves have undoubtedly had some form of experience in this respect, or know of someone who has. Cases of actual physical healing associated with prayer, substantiated by medical doctors, are many. Most people, however, like the Biblical "doubting Thomas," remain skeptical until they have firsthand experience. Experience. after all, is the highest authority, taking precedence over all bibles, scriptures, theories, etc. Like many people, the authors also prefer to retain a healthy objectivity in evaluating cases of answers to prayer healing or otherwise. Yet, when a case is thrust upon us, we find great difficulty in not believing that some superpersonal force is at work. Such was the case with the wife of a minister with whom we are associated. Mrs. G. is a classic case of the person for whom the doctors had done everything medically possible. Her kidney was so degenerated that she was actually passing pieces of its tissue in her urine. In 1970 she attended a meeting of the healing minister Katherine Kulhmann at the Washington Hilton Hotel.

> Being a minister's wife, I was somewhat self-conscious at being in such a meeting. I had taken a seat in the very back of the room, but was approached by a woman who was a stranger to me, asking if I would like to have her seat near the front of the room since she had to leave. She led me down to the seat. During the healing Mrs. Kulhmann proceeded up the aisle asking that people who desired healing stretch their arms into the air. I was reluctant to make this display, but suddenly found my arms outstretched into the air. That is the last thing I remember until coming to, lying on the floor with a blanket covering me and Mrs. Kulhmann leaning over me telling me that I had been healed. When I returned to my doctor, the x-rays showed my kidney to be completely whole and healed. His exact words to me were, "If you ever come back into this office with a kidney ailment, it will be as a completely new case."

This woman recently related her story to our congregation at Riverside Church in Washington, D.C. We knew her before and after she was healed. Another woman of our acquaintance, who also related her story at Riverside, described how her husband was afflicted by palsy of the hand. As the two of them knelt praying holding hands, his hand suddenly completely stopped shaking and never started again. There are, of course, literally thousands of cases such as these.

COMMUNICATION WITH THE DEAD

This probably is the least believable of all psychic activity and phenomena. Yet, again we are faced with thousands of seemingly authentic cases. As with the records of most of the other phenomena described in this chapter, the records of purported communication with the dead extend from antiquity to modern times. The best-known record in history comes again from the New Testament, concerning the resurrection of Jesus who was reportedly seen several times by various people after his death. In modern times, no less a personage than Dr. Norman Vincent Peale reports having communicated with both his mother and his brother after their deaths. In a book entitled *Thirty Years Among The Dead*, Carl A. Wickland reported scores of cases purporting communications with disembodied spirits. Edgar Cayce also reported numerous cases of communication with the dead and spirit forms of some kind, as did Bishop James J. Pike. Arthur Ford and others.

Most so-called communication with the dead or with the spirit world takes place in the presence of or through a psychic medium. A medium is a person who, for some reason, presumably has an extra sensitivity to the spiritual realm. Usually some form of trance or seance is involved, during which a departed spirit manifests itself. Most of the time, these sittings take place in the presence of several witnesses. Spirits manifest themselves in a variety of ways— speaking, showing themselves, speaking through the medium, "possessing" the body of the medium, or moving physical objects. A photographer named Hans Holzer has obtained what appears to be photographic proof of the existence of both spirits and the possibility of their manifesting themselves. In a book entitled *Psychic Photography: Threshold of a New Science*, McGraw-Hill, 1969, he has published numerous pictures of "spirits" taken under, so far as can be determined, fraud-proof conditions.

Even if there is no such thing as communication with the dead, there is sufficient evidence of some form of "spirit world" to warrant an attempt at investigation and explanation. If such an invisible realm exists, it would most definitely seem to lie at least partially outside of the normal intrapersonal powers of the individual mind, and therefore within the realm of the concept of the superconscious.

TELEPATHY—TELEPORTATION—TELEKINESIS

Telepathy is the communication between human beings, over varying distances, by direct mental contact, without spoken word or any other form of physical or sensory communication. Teleportation is the capability of a person to move his own body through mental power alone. There are many apparently well-substantiated cases on record throughout history and in modern times. Perhaps the best-known examples are those recorded in the New Testament, such as the following:

> So when they had rowed about five and twenty or thirty furlongs they saw Jesus walking on the water . . .
>
> *John 6:19*

> And when he had spoken these things, while they beheld, he [Jesus] was taken up; and a cloud received him out of their sight.
>
> *Acts 1:9*

Another form of this type of activity is known as *astralprojection*, the capability of a person to leave his own body in a spirit form and to move about, capable of observing his own body and aware of the fact that he has left it. In a book entitled *Out-of-Body Experiences*, a psychic researcher named Suzy Smith has compiled a rather extensive collection of numerous apparently well-documented cases of this type of activity. There seems, in fact, to be an upsurge today in the scientific inquiry into and reporting of this fascinating realm of human behavior. More and more books are lately being published on the subject. It is up to the reader, of course, to decide for himself just how valid and well-substantiated such documentation is. Our main purpose here is one of delineation. We will, however, go so far as to say that it is quite unlikely that so many reports of so many cases by so many people do not bear some evidence of the existence of some kind of superconscious realm or activity.

Further, many of these psychic experiences involving such phenomena as leaving the body, seeing mentally over distances, clairvoyance, etc., are definitely dreamlike in nature—giving some rise to the possibility that they are definitely connected with the unconscious as well as with any mental power that may extend beyond the person of the individual. We would merely again provide our basic warning and guideline: be constantly alert to *all* possibilities, keep good records, and exhaust all possibilities for ordinary interpretation before progressing to the possibility of the extraordinary.

SUMMARY

One must conclude that there is some evidence for the existence of a division or part of the human psyche and its capabilities such as the superconscious. The accounts of such activities as telepathy, clairvoyance, mind control, precognition—even communication with the dead and the working of the so-called Holy Spirit—are numerous. How does man begin to tap the resources of the superconscious that apparently are available to him? At least a part of the answer seems to lie in a greater identification with the energies of one's own superconscious—one's own higher mental and spiritual being. It is quite likely that the entry point is through listening to one's dreams and the "voices." Artists, writers, mystics, philosophers and other creative persons have been aware of these possibilities for generations. Persons who have tapped this resource have been able to "seed" the atmospheres around themselves with healing and wholeness. In the words of the noted theologian,

Martin Buber, "We have only to reach out to the universe with our arms to find the other arms which surround the universe grasping ours."

*Sir, do not mock our dreamers . . .
their words become the deeds of
freedom.*

Heinrich Heine

10
Summary of Common Types of Dreams

Most dreams fall into certain broad categories. As a part of your base for sorting and interpreting the contents of your own unconscious, it will help to keep in mind what these categories are. Remember, however that the meaning of your dream cannot be found by simply seeing if it matches what someone else's dream means. The purpose here is not to give you a catalog from which to assign your own dream a "classification" or "type." It is rather to provide you another insight into what your dream can or is *likely* to mean. Do not worry, either, if a particular dream you might have does not fit neatly into one of these categories, or seems to fit more than one. As do most other things in the human experience, these groupings overlap and intermix with each other. The best approach is simply to add the following information to your general understanding of dreams, and then to examine the contents of your own dreams with this information in mind.

We have already considered several major categories or types of dreams. For convenience, we shall begin by summarizing these:

The Shadow Dream: This is probably the most common type—or at least a great many of your dreams will contain shadow figures. There is a simple twofold reason for this. First, there is no human being who does not have more than one self or aspect to his or her personality. These selves are always present and share all of the experiences of the conscious and of the other selves. Second, the dream is primarily a self-experience, and one's selves naturally will be the most frequent participants in it. As we have seen, the shadow figure basically represents a negative, neglected or underdeveloped part of the personality—or a positive, wiser, or more astute part of the personality. In either case, its appearance in a dream usually signifies that it is not being sufficiently heard, taken into account or given attention in conscious life, and therefore is trying to assert itself or obtain the required attention through the unconscious in the dream. The shadow may offer guidance, additional reasoning or decision-making power, or issue a warning that if a certain set of conditions persists there "may be trouble."

The Persona Dream: With an understanding of shadow figures and how they function, comes an understanding of other figures and how they function. Persona figures, too, represent parts of the personality. They behave similarly to shadow figures. The main difference is that they represent *external* parts of the personality as opposed to internal parts. They are also known as functional complexes because they are devised by the human personality to perform some function in the external world. As we have seen, the main danger associated with the personas is that the person may become overidentified with one or more of them and thus lose his own most essential sense of identity and being.

The Anima Dream: With the anima dream, we begin to speak of the collective unconscious as opposed to the personal unconscious. The anima is the image of femaleness, or the woman part, present in every male. It, too, behaves much like the shadow figure. It always appears in female form, but not always as a human figure. It manifests itself in a way that shows its present state within the psychological makeup of the dreamer. The main danger associated with the anima is similar to that associated with the persona; namely, that of neglect or underdevelopment—or conversely, of overdevelopment.

The Animus Dream: The animus is the image of maleness, or the male part of the female personality. In dreams, the animus behaves in the same way as the anima behaves in males.

The Archetypal Dream: This is the expression of a deep, nonpersonal sensing, urging, awareness or image that arises out of the inherited, collective experience of the individual person as a member of the human race. Both the anima and animus dreams are classed as archetypal, since they originate out of the same type of inherited experience. The archetypal dream is often related to mythology or legend, because these are in fact often the expression of the same, inherited experiences and capabilities to perceive the universal. It should be particularly remembered that the archetype is not the *idea itself*, but represents the *capability* within each person to produce the idea. Probably the best source of identification of the personal archetypal dream is the Bible, because it is more available to the average reader. It also is probably the most comprehensive collection of archetypal experiences to be found in a single, compact place.

The Superconscious Dream: This is probably the least comprehended of all of the dream types, but there is definite evidence that it—or something like it—occurs in the human dream experience. Basically, this type of dream activity relates to that which cannot be explained in terms of the conscious, or the personal or collective unconscious experience. It is the experience that, so far as is known or observable, seems to come from *outside* of the person. Included in this category are such experiences as the clairvoyant, the so-called "vision," astralprojection and similar experiences. Such occurrences, of course, must be approached with extreme caution from the standpoint of their validity. One must consider all other possibilities before attributing the contents of a given dream to any of these phenomenon. Although presumed transpersonal dream activity has been reported for many centuries, it is only recently that any work has been done to try to submit the experiences to any scientifically controlled observation. Caution and objectivity are the watchwords here.

OTHER DREAM CLASSIFICATIONS

In one sense, when you understand the "figure dreams" described in the foregoing chapters and summarized above, you have a pretty good understanding of dream typology. You can, however, gain additional insight by taking other cross sections, as it were. Dreams might, for example, also be classified according to the time-frame with which they deal or seem to deal, for example, past, present or future. They might also be classified in terms of the "messages" that they bear. Or, they might be classified in terms of the emotional temperaments that they represent.

One of the best ways to gain insight into the various possible types of dream activity is simply to recount in your mind the various types of thinking and feeling activity you are capable of in conscious life. For your unconscious mind is not really that much different. If you can wonder about the future in conscious life, you can do the same in your unconscious. If you can experience fear, anxiety, hate, frustration, etc., at the conscious level, you can also experience it at the unconscious level. If, in the evening, you can simply take account of the day's, week's or year's activity in your waking mind, you can do so in your sleeping mind, too. The main difference, as we have already seen, is that your unconscious mind is not as restricted as your conscious in terms of making things fit into logical sequence, obeying the laws of space or social decorum. For example, while still fully clothed in conscious life, you may feel naked and denuded. You may wish you could get "above it all." You may wrestle with a problem or be preoccupied recurrently with some circumstance, or merely imagine things and fantasize. All such things go on in your conscious mind daily and constantly, and you can clearly see that they are mental activity, not physical facts. The big difference in the unconscious is that these things *are the reality*. In any case, simply viewing the types of activity that go on in your conscious will give you a similar view of the possible typology in your unconscious dream activity. Following are the main examples:

The Anxiety Dream

Who is not anxious about something these days? Man fears everything from death to loss of face. It would be inconceivable that this anxiety would not "seep down" into the unconscious. Therefore, a dream may be nothing more than the expression of some anxiety. Depending on their intensity, some anxiety dreams may give rise to the familiar description of "nightmare." Following are some typical anxiety dreams:

— A business executive dreams that an important document on which he and his staff have been working for a month is stolen or lost.
— A high school student dreams that she fails her English examination.
— A housewife dreams that one of her children is hit by a car.
— A ten-year-old child dreams that an airplane bombs his home.

Examination of such dreams as these reveals that their interpretation is not so terribly difficult. What else might this businessman be thinking about these days, or the high school student? Is not the mother recurrently concerned with such matters as these? And the child is so constantly exposed to the news of violence and bombing on his home television set that it is no wonder that he would become anxious and that his mind would be full of such thoughts. The interesting thing is that even in relatively şimple anxiety dreams such as these, there often may be an inherent warning. Many anxiety dreams are indications that something constructive should be done. For, it is a safe bet that this executive will take perhaps an added security precaution with his precious document. The mother may issue that extra word of warning as the child departs for school the next morning. And the student may take that "life-saving" last look at his notes before his exam. The child? Perhaps it will be this very dream that ultimately leads him to a pacifist role in later life. We must come to a fuller understanding of how such apparently disconnected, seemingly phantasmagorical experiences actually intermingle with "real" life. For then the "scales" fall away from our eyes and we begin to see the true synchronicity of all events in life, and that there truly is no separation between what goes on inside or outside us.

The Happy Dream

We would not have you believe that all dreams are sombre and sinister in content and meaning. All are not anxieties and warnings. Just as your conscious mind is capable of humor, satire, feelings of well being, etc., so is your unconscious. The prospective bride, for example, dreams of the beauty of her wedding. The young man finds himself laughing uncontrollably at some fantastically humorous experience in his dream, the child romps and plays. The man who falls asleep with peace and rectitude within his heart in all probability will experience the same in his inner world. But there is a deeper meaning here too. If you would be at peace in your dreams, you must be at peace in your waking self as well. The question may be: If I am capable of celebrating life in my dreams, am I also capable of celebrating it while I am awake? Or, are my dreams merely compensation for what is missing in waking life?

The Wish Fulfillment Dream

Some psychologists mistakenly assume that *all* dreams are merely the fulfillment of desires that cannot be fulfilled in waking life. This is not true. Some dreams, however, do fall into this category. Most of the time, however, if a dream is compensatory in this way—if it is a fulfillment of what cannot be done or experienced in waking life—the dreamer should begin to take a closer look at whether or not his waking life is what it ought to be. If, for example, you dream of flying, it might be well to see what in your conscious life you are trying to "get above." If you dream that you are living in a luxurious mansion, perhaps it is the luxurious feeling that is missing in your waking life. Perhaps, also, that luxurious feeling in its truest and purest form may not come from actually living in a real mansion but in living in one of the spiritual "many mansions" that Jesus mentioned to his disciples.

The wish fulfillment dream also may represent something that goes far back into the dreamer's life, perhaps to a repressed childhood desire. One must always remember that to the unconscious, there is no passage of time. And the desires and life-shortcomings of childhood are as real within it today as if they had happened but a moment before. One of the secrets of adjustment to mature life, in fact, is to recognize and come to terms with the lackings and shortcomings of earlier life. It is to come to a true sense of exactly who and what you are and how you came to be the person that you are today. It is to see that there is no need to feel guilty or neglected, to feel self-pity, as if you have been "left out" of the benefits of life simply because of something that is missing in your early life. The time is now! Living in the present is one of the major keys to being a mature person.

The "Postdictive" Dream

In a sense, almost all dreams are "post-dictive"; that is, they "state something that has happened in the past." A more specific meaning is intended here, however. Some dreams fall into the category of merely being a recounting or synopsis, a kind of summing up of things that have happened. Remember that the unconscious mind, among other things, is the master historian, the archivist of all your experiences. Sometimes, depending on your current waking state, it may simply engage in a "taking of accounts." It will be rare, however, that you will not be able to derive some message from taking stock of your dreams. The simple listing out of events and information usually leads to some conclusion as to how things could, should, or may be.

The Predictive Dream

One of the most common questions that people ask about dreams is: "Can they predict the future?" The answer is yes, provided that one understands the nature of that prediction. As seen in Chapter 9, there are dreams that definitely seem to be clear-cut cases of foretelling future events. But we speak here of the average predictive personal dream. In these cases, the prediction is more in the form of a reasoning process that takes place in the unconscious. It is a determination of high probability. That is, there is nothing "magical" or "supernatural" about the predictive qualities of the dream. This can be seen in the cases of the young man who dreamed of being pushed off a cliff and of the man who dreamed of robbing the bank and getting caught.

The key to interpretation almost invariably will lie in the ability to translate the images and symbols selected by the unconscious to illustrate the results of its reasoning. A woman, for example, dreamed that her stomach had been cut open and worried in the dream about being infected through the wound. Upon examination of her conscious life, it was found that she was on a "crash" diet. It was almost certain that this dream was predicting to her that she was weakening the condition of her body and opening it to possible infection.

Another young woman dreamed that she had lost her cat and was searching for it. In many cases, dreaming of an animal has something to do with the primitive sensualities of the dreamer, because this is what animals basically represent in life—the unreasoned, physical, often purely sexual aspects of living. This is the level at which animals live. But in this particular case, the girl had a very close relationship with her pet. In fact, it probably came under the classification of "family." When we asked her who Misty (the cat) was, what she represented, the girl quickly replied, "Oh, she's love, and closeness, and warmth—I love her very much." Other things in this girl's life revealed that Misty was just about the only "person" with whom she had such a loving relationship. In most of the rest of her living, this girl existed on a purely mechanistic level. She was highly judgmental of people, often irritable with them, preoccupied with many superficial things, etc. Yet, underneath, she was clearly capable of the loving relationship, as her love of the cat showed. The predictive qualities of this dream are not hard to see. The losing of Misty represents her fear that she may lose the things that Misty represents—love, companionship and closeness. Her inner self is telling her that she is on a course in life that can lead to the loss. The necessity for constructive action is inherent in the dream content.

Body or Health Dream

It would be less than realistic to assume that the mind which exists in a body does not have some awareness of what is going on in that body. A young man with whom we recently counseled reported to us several dreams of a recurring nature. He consistently dreamed of being shut up in closely confined places such as coffins and small cells. Always, he experienced the sensation of suffocating. Always, too, as he sat in the counseling room, he chain-smoked cigarette after cigarette. It was not too difficult for us to determine that his body in fact was literally crying out for air. We finally talked him into giving up the habit, and his dreams disappeared totally.

Frequently, the dream concerned with health and body is definitely predictive in nature. That is, the unconscious seems to know what may happen with its own body before the conscious is aware. There are many cases of this on record going back to ancient times. In ancient Greece the god of healing was Aesculapius, in whose honor many temples were built and in which physicians of the day practiced their art. The sick and ailing were brought to the temple for treatment. There are many stories in mythology of how the physicians diagnosed illnesses and prescribed treatments based on interpretation of their patients' dreams. Physical treatment based on dreams is not limited to the past. Numerous people today dream of both impending illnesses and often the necessary treatments for their cure. Edgar Cayce recorded the cases of hundreds of patients whose illnesses were revealed through dreams. These cases are a matter of documented record and cannot be denied. One woman, for example, dreamed that "I went into the bathroom and urinated. In the toilet I saw little red monsters." Previously, there had been no knowledge of any disease or ailment. Yet, within a week, this woman was diagnosed as having a bladder infection. A young man reported to the authors the following dream:

> I saw a little female dog with a wounded and bandaged paw. I went to the dog to comfort it. As I reached out for the paw, the dog turned into a little girl with a bandaged hand. The child became frightened and ran from me. I ran after her. She ran into some bushes. As I approached the bushes I realized that she had turned into a vicious small animal such as a mink or vixen. She snarled at me and started to attack me as I approached her. I awoke quite frightened.

This dream is most interesting from several points of view. To the experienced interpreter, among other things, it is clearly an anima dream. It is a dream closely linked with the pronounced sensual nature of the dreamer. But perhaps even more significantly, it seems almost definitely to have turned out as a health-related predictive dream. For at the time, the dreamer felt that he was in absolutely perfect health. Yet, within a week, he developed a fever and chills, went to the doctor and found that he had an infection of his sexual organs.

Many times, dreams related to the body and health will actually contain specific references to the parts of the body involved. Elsie Sechrist, author of *Dreams, Your Magic Mirror*, an account of the life of Edgar Cayce, reports several of these well-documented cases. In almost every one, prior to the dream, the dreamer was totally unaware that anything was wrong with his or her body. Yet, within a matter of a few days or weeks after the dream, medical diagnosis confirmed something wrong with the particular part of the body involved in the dream. There simply are too many provable cases on record to ignore the possibility of the real-life relationship of this type of dream. In any case, it would seem a much safer approach for anyone who dreams of a specific part of his own body, regardless of whether anything actually seems to be wrong, to get a medical diagnosis.

The Sensory Experience Dream

Closely related to the body and health dream is what we have come to call the sensory experience dream. Recall that the unconscious uses the same set of senses that the conscious, waking mind and body use. Some dreams represent an experiencing of what the senses are perceiving either while the dreamer sleeps or what the senses have experienced just before falling asleep. Take, for example, the dreamer who dreams that his house is burning, or perhaps that he is witnessing a fire—or even visiting a hell-like place. Upon awakening, he realizes that he has been sleeping too close to a heater or in an overheated room. Perhaps, he dreams that he is carrying a ponderous weight only to awaken and find that there are too many blankets on his bed, or that a pet has gotten into his bedroom and is sleeping on his body. Then there are, of course, sexual dreams; for example, the "wet dreams" frequently experienced by young men, or even older men who are deprived of normal waking sexual relationships. So the sensory dream may also be compensatory in nature. We should point out here, also, that there is no need for the dreamer to feel guilty about any such dreams, although many people often do. There should never be any necessity for self-recrimination for things within one's makeup that are perfectly natural and human mechanisms for maintaining the equilibrium of the whole self.

The Plea Dream

We have already implied the nature of this type of dream and merely include it here to make this summary complete. This is what many dreams are: They are pleas from some part of the personality for attention or for a more equitable inclusion in the total life of the dreamer. Another way of putting it is to think of them as a maintenance of the "tension of opposites." In fact, this is what much of the self-adjustive mechanism of the human psyche is all about. We are all so inherently dualistic in so many ways, so polarized in our natures, that the maintenance of that polarity is a natural function of our beings. "For every action, there is a reaction" is a fundamental law of nature. In many ways, when the tension of opposites ceases, life itself ceases.

The Recriminatory Dream

Generally speaking, the unconscious is much more puritanically moral than is the conscious. In other words, it may often "preach" to its owner. It may cajole and even "nag" him to do what it knows is best. It is, as it were, the parent, the voice of conscience, even at times the voice of what some religionists would call the "holy spirit" of God. A person can do worse than to listen to these inner voices, whatever he or she chooses to call them.

The Nonsense Dream

This represents one of the differences between the authors' approach to dream interpretation and the approaches of many other theorists and practitioners. We do not close the door, as it were, on *any* of the possibilities regarding dreams and their interpretation. This includes the possibility that there may be no meaning or useful information in the contents of some dreams. That is, some dreams may be nothing more than mere nonsense, having no real significance in the life of the dreamer. If one is to remain *completely* open-minded in this respect, of course, one would also have to ask *why* the nonsense. Is there too much of it? Does it represent the possibility that the dreamer is hiding or trying to escape from the more serious considerations of life? That is, in other words, the very existence of nonsense, although it may have no meaning of itself, may have meaning and significance. We do doubt, therefore, that any dream can be truly meaningless.

The Recurring Dream

This is not a category per se, for any dream of any type can be a recurring dream. Basically, when a certain dream or type of dream repeats itself, this means that that particular aspect of the dreamer's life or personality is even more demanding of attention or adjustment. When the dream recurs, it obviously takes on added significance. Something inside the person most definitely wants to be heard and dealt with.

SUMMARY

These, then, are the major classifications of types of dreams—or at least one way of classifying them. Knowing them constitutes one more step in the development of the individual knowledge base and awareness necessary to deriving some structured meaning from one's own unconscious and its activity.

11
Getting Started

The assumption in this chapter is that you have decided
to embark upon a serious program of realistic dream interpretation. Such a program, of course, can go on for a long time
if you so desire—all the rest of your life if you want it to. If
you have absorbed the material presented in the
foregoing chapters, you are ready to begin such a program.
As you progress, you will gain experience and insight into
the "territory" in which you are operating (your own
psyche) and see how the things said in this book are borne
out in your own personal dreams. Very quickly, you will
begin to see the real significance of your dreams in your
overall life. Increasingly then, you will see how to use the
information that you obtain from them in working out a
more satisfactory way of personal living. You will see how
paying attention to your dreams can lead you closer to
some or all the following ideals:
  — Deeper insight into your own being and behavior
  — Better understanding of your family and other
    people around you

- Greater inner peace and harmony
- Greater personal creativity
- Fuller insight and intuition
- More appreciation of life's experiences
- Better physical rest and well-being
- A deeper and richer spiritual life
- Greater wisdom and connection with the universal truths

Such things, of course, will not come overnight. But they will come to the person who assiduously applies himself to better understanding of his inner, unconscious being and living. Like most other things in life, too, they are more likely to come to the person who proceeds in an organized and planned way. Toward this end, following are some basic guidelines for developing your own ongoing program of personal dream interpretation. Use these in conjunction with the information given in Chapter 12.

KEEP A WRITTEN RECORD

This is the first and most important thing that you need. If you have not already begun, start now to keep a daily diary of your dreams. Do not merely scribble notes, for ultimately you will accumulate a considerable amount of material. You might as well begin from the outset to keep this information in good order. Figure 11-1 shows a basic format for entries in your daily diary. If some other format is more convenient for you to use, use it. But your daily entries should contain at least the information shown.

Date: Use the date of the morning after the dream.

Complete or Fragment: Some mental block may prevent you from remembering an entire dream. So record this fact. For, as you become more intimately acquainted with your own unconcious and less fearful of probing it, more will be revealed to you, and you will be able to fit various pieces of information together.

DREAM DIARY SHEET

☐ Complete Dream ☐ Fragment   Date _____

Description of Conscious Self

Type of Dream

Setting and Time

Narrative of Dream

OBJECTS AND SYMBOLS		
Description	General Meaning (Chapter 12)	My Meaning

CHARACTERS AND FIGURES		
The Character or Figure	Meaning	Type

Pre-Dream Situation

Awakening Thoughts and Feeling

My Interpretation of the Dream

Figure 11-1. A Dream Diary Sheet

Description of Conscious Self: As already mentioned, your conscious self almost invariably will be present in your dream as the observer or audience. You may on occasion find, however, that this part of you in the dream also has some revelatory characteristics or does some things that will provide insight. For example, what is the attitude of your conscious self toward what is going on in the dream? Are you fearful? Is there a sense of well-being? Is the whole conscious self present? Perhaps there is a limb missing, or some distortion of the body, for instance, is it larger or smaller? Are you your present age? Are you your own sex? Are you well or ill? What is your relationship to the action: are you participating or merely observing? The answers to such questions will obviously reveal much and often will establish the basic flavor of the whole interpretation.

Type of Dream: This again is basic information. If you can clearly establish what category the dream falls into, specific contents and symbology will fall more clearly into place. For convenience, here are the types as we have described them:

- The Shadow Dream
- The Persona Dream
- The Anima or Animus Dream
- The Archetypal Dream
- The Superconscious Dream
- The Anxiety Dream (including nightmares)
- The Happy Dream
- The Wish Fulfillment Dream
- The Postdictive Dream
- The Predictive Dream (including warnings)
- The Body or Health Dream
- The Sensory Experience Dream
- The Plea Dream (recall the tension of opposites)
- The Recriminatory Dream

— The Nonsense Dream

Remember too that these types are not hard and fast categories; they are merely intended as guidelines to help you identify the nature of your dream.

Setting and Time: Observe carefully the setting and time. The time frame within the dream provides important clues to such matters as your hidden desires, to how you really view yourself and to how you generally regard yourself (whether or not you know this in conscious life). For example, if the dream takes place in your childhood, you would almost immediately know that somewhere in you there is a need or desire to return to this time. If the dream time is unidentifiable, this is important too. For you may be dealing with something more universal. If the action is in another time in history, this also will yield valuable clues as to your associations, needs and desires.

The setting is important for similar reasons. If the action is at your place of work or in your own home, for example, this establishes the basic tenor of the interpretation. If the scene is in a totally unknown place, you have an entirely different set of interpretive conditions. Is the setting real or imaginary? Perhaps you may even visit hell as Dante did, or the mystical Wonderland or Land of Oz, a place where "wishes come true." Are you in an airplane, on the ground, on water, in a house? What kind of house is it? Is it a great mansion, a hovel, a cave? Are you above or below the earth? Are you in a city, in the country? The possibilities are obviously too numerous to list. But when you clearly see the setting, you immediately have important symbolic information.

Narrative of Dream: Tell here the plot and action within the dream in as much detail as you can remember. Place special emphasis on remembering *who* does *what* to *whom*. Remember that a great many of the characters in your dream actually are representations of *you*. Therefore, this will give you insight into your own inner conflicts and the interrelationships of your many selves. Look for other action, too. For example, during the action is there music playing, is there traffic passing by, is it raining, are there groups of people doing other things besides the main action in which you (your conscious self), the observer, are seeing or participating in? Is someone else besides you conversing, or playing, or walking or running? Are you riding in a vehicle? What kind of vehicle is it? Are you fishing, or playing, or escaping, or laughing, or crying? All of these are symbolic actions in your dream. All are important. All are data for evaluation.

Objects and Symbols: These obviously relate to the setting of the dream. List every inanimate object that you can remember. For example, if you are writing something, list the implement with which you are writing as well as what you are writing on. If there is a table set with food, list each item of food that you can specifically recall. Even list the items of clothing that people are wearing if you can remember them. If you are in a boat, take specific note of what kind of rowing or paddling implements are present. If you are in a room, note specific items of furniture, paintings, toys, tools, etc. Items such as money, water, vehicles, plant life, shapes, colors, weapons, etc., all frequently have a high symbolic and interpretive value. It was highly significant, for example, that the butcher knife in the dream of the young woman described earlier came from her own kitchen. For this gave a clue that it was she who held it in the character of her shadow figure. Or, suppose that you are trying to row a boat with oars that have holes in them, or with a stick instead of an oar. It takes very little interpretative ability in such a case to see that the futility of rowing with such an implement may have some bearing upon the feelings of the dreamer or his life situation. (See Chapter 12 for further discussion of objects and symbols.)

Characters and Figures: List every character that appears in the dream. Then describe how each appears as fully as you can recall. Then identify each as to whether you think it was a shadow, one of your persona, your anima or animus, etc. As you actually write down an objective description of the characteristics of these people, you will quickly come to realize, to make the sometimes startling discovery, that many of these people actually are *you*. You will find yourself appearing in many guises— simply because there are many you's. You may, for example, see a policeman admonishing you not to do something—strictly and harshly. You may see the glittering, scintillating personality that you wish you were riding in a fine limousine in wealth and splendor. You will see pompous, pseudo-sophisticated, "phony" people. You will see little children cringing in fear at the mysteries of life. You will see frightened, pitiful creatures running to escape from troubles and conflicts. Occasionally, too, you may see the courageous, decisive individual who does not turn and run from life's paradoxes, conflicts and decisions. And, as you make friends with these characters, and learn to walk hand-in-hand with them, you will find yourself in conscious life standing more and more on your own two feet. You will be able to face life situations, evaluating them, surmounting many that are now defeating you. And those that you do not surmount you will face with greater courage, and be better able to face and conquer their negative consequences.

Pre-Dream Situation: Recall how we have stressed the importance of the total perspective. Your dream fits into a larger picture, and must be interpreted in these terms. Therefore, you should have a written record of your current psychic situation for comparison with your dream material. It may not be necessary to record this for every dream entry, for the simple reason that it will not necessarily vary as much as your dreams will. It probably will be sufficient to do this only periodically, perhaps on a weekly or monthly basis. A good practice is to have a "stock-taking" once a month. Thus, as your dream log or diary develops, interspersed every thirty days or so may be a separate sheet synopsizing your current waking situation. In your daily entry you may merely state a few key words such as "April situation unchanged," or "went to sleep generally anxious because of office situation . . . or family situation . . . or Mary's problem," etc.

Awakening Thoughts and Feelings: Having a record of how you feel about what has occurred in your dream is important. If you awaken in a frightened state, there is a reason for it. Or, you might awaken from a dream with a feeling of well-being, that everything is going to be all right. Call these premonitions, if you like. But they are more likely to be indications that you are making progress in confronting and embracing certain of your inner figures, or overcoming conflicts. Listen to these feelings within you, for your dreams do help and guide you. Conversely, if you awaken from a dream with a definite feeling of foreboding, do not hesitate to take an extra precaution with respect to whatever the foreboding applies to. Extra precautions rarely do any harm. And they are likely to save a lot of trouble and grief. There are many, many cases of this on record. If, for example, you dream of some trouble in a certain part of your body, treat it seriously. Do not become a hypo-chondriac, but do take note. If you dream of losing some-thing of value, either in terms of material things or personal relationships, take a second look at the situation in waking life. Perhaps something in waking life has "seeped down" into your unconscious. Maybe some other person has been broadcasting subtle clues to trouble in a relationship that your conscious did not pick up, but your unconscious did. Most important, however, as you record your waking feelings day after day, you will come to see patterns in the state of your emotional well-being. You will see whether you are growing, slipping backward, or remaining stagnant. And, more often than not, you will know what to do simply because you are aware of your problems.

Your Interpretation: Finally, based on all of the things we have said throughout this book, write down what the dream *means to you*. Do not worry too much about what it may mean to someone else. In fact, unless you happen to be closely associated with someone else who takes his dream life seriously, you probably will be better off not discussing your interpretations. After all, you are out to understand and improve the inner, private you. The results of this understanding and improvement will soon enough become obvious to the outside world. And it is these results that you are after.

We do not, however, negate the soundness and profitability of discussing the contents of your dreams with others. For this activity can lead to even further insight. You will find the serious and intelligent evaluations of other people also of value in "putting it all together." All we are saying is that you should choose your confidants cautiously—which is obviously good advice for any realm of life.

In summary, you should be able to see that what you are trying to do in keeping a daily dream diary is to develop as complete a profile as you can of your conscious and unconscious activity. If you already keep a diary or journal, there is no reason that your dream diary cannot be incorporated as a part of it. In fact, it should be. For, if up until now you have merely been keeping a record of the things that go on in your waking life, you really have only a *partial* record. Finally, if it has not already become obvious, we have been talking here of a *serious* effort toward self-understanding and self-improvement. We realize that this sort of effort is not for everyone. Dream interpretation is not a parlor game.

ADDITIONAL HINTS

Following are some additional guidelines and suggestions that can help you to obtain fuller clarity and meaning in the interpretation of your dreams:

Personal History: It is not a bad idea to begin your dream diary with a kind of synopsis of your personal history to date. This should be quite private and you need not show it to anyone. Make this evaluation honest and realistic. Do not hide from the truth about yourself. If in your present life you truly think that you have arrived at a fair measure of maturity and decision-making capability, by all means say so. But do not pretend to yourself. If you have deep and abiding fears and frustrations, so state them to yourself. Develop a true and accurate present profile of the person that you now are, how you really see yourself. You may do this in any way that you like, but we suggest that this profile contain at least the following information.

Who am I? Exactly how do I think of myself as fitting into the life around me? How do others see me as opposed to what I really am? What are my various personas, the masks that I wear in society? How do these differ from what I really am? Am I basically a courageous or a cowardly person? Am I facing life in a mature and decisive way? Do I actually have a plan for successful living? Am I a compassionate person? Am I selfish? Am I childish? What are my main problems in facing and dealing with life successfully?

Where do I come from? What has made me the way I am today? Do I feel basically inferior and unsure of myself? Why? What has happened in my past life that makes me feel this way? Am I any different than I was a year ago today? Or, do I still have the same fears and anxieties that I had then? Have I grown and matured any in the last year?

Where am I going? Do I have a plan for living? Do I know what I really want out of life? Can I sit down and make a clear-cut list of the things I want most from life in the order of their priority? What are the ten things I want most out of life? What have I done or am I doing to actually get them? Are they merely wishes, or goals toward which I am realistically working? Where will I be a year from today? What will I be?

These are not all of the questions that you can answer in your personal profile, but if you answer just these few, and if you answer them with true honesty, you will have a pretty good picture of the person that is presently you. Remember, too, that no amount of hiding from or "sugar-coating" your shortcomings and faults will make them disappear.

Getting Ready to Dream: At the end of Chapter 4, we listed eleven preliminary suggestions for preparing yourself to dream. You can pretty much tailor this sort of thing to suit your own personality and natural inclinations. You basically are after the necessary inner openness, awareness and receptiveness that will enable you to do the following:

1. Be an efficient observer within your own dreams
2. Remember what you dream
3. Intentionally and purposefully participate in your own dreams
4. Control the actions of your conscious self within your dreams, for example, in confronting and embracing your shadow figures.

Of course, these capabilities will not come to you overnight. They must be cultivated and developed; you must train yourself to have them. So do not be discouraged if you cannot immediately do the things that we suggest here. Just keep trying and persistently practicing. Soon, you will find yourself doing things that you never "dreamed" you could do.

Use Autosuggestion. Suggest strongly to yourself every night as you fall asleep that not only will you remember what you dream, but that you are keenly and anxiously anticipating the things that you will see and experience as you dream. Fall asleep with this feeling of receptiveness foremost in your mind. More than this, have faith and trust in your inner self. Do not be afraid or worry that you will not be able to handle what goes on in your dreams. It is far better to make the attempt to deal with what will occur, since it will occur whether you try to deal with it or not. You are on the safer side by directly confronting and going forward into whatever will happen as opposed to cringing from it. No harm will come to you.

Use Meditative Technique. A transition from meditation to dreaming is one of the most natural ones that you could make, for the two are highly similar in structure and action. This is why we suggested that you use some object or picture, real or imagined, concentrate on it and project yourself forward into whatever you are visualizing. This has the net effect of focusing your attentions and shutting out irrelevancies, making it easier to concentrate on the upcoming events in your dream.

Be a Good Observer. Soon you will find that you actually can be a purposeful observer within your dream. You will find a developing awareness of the connection between your conscious self in waking and the same self in dreaming. This is when your memory after awakening will begin to improve.

Converse-Befriend-Embrace: This already has been mentioned. Basically you want to develop a personal attitude toward the figures and events in your dreams that will enable you to face and understand them instead of fleeing from them. If you see a dead person in your dream, for example, do not be afraid of him or her. This is not a "ghost." In all probability, it is merely the best representation that your unconscious could find for something that it is trying to tell you, usually some aspect of your self. Your approach here should be to try to converse with the person. Ask him what he wants. Come right out in your dream and say, "What do you want? What are you trying to tell me? How can I help you?" The figure may not answer you. Or, it may merely answer you with actions instead of words. If, for example, it reaches toward you as if to grab or embrace you, hold out your hand or arms and welcome it.

Also, if you find yourself an observer of some action, try going forward into it in an inquisitive and honestly questioning way. Participate if you can. For example, it would have been extremely interesting and revelatory had the young woman in the dream cited in Chapter 5 approached the girl-child on the stairs, or simply turned and asked the figure beside her why the child was frightened of her, or why she was trying to kill the child or the dreamer.

The Unusual Message. If you receive an unusual message in a dream, see some symbol that doesn't immediately make sense, or something that doesn't seem decipherable, there are a couple of things that you can do. First, recount your waking life to see if there is something to which the symbol relates. Second, before your next sleep, ponder this item and suggest to yourself that tonight you are going to try to seek the answer. Decide that you will go back into the same dream and find out what it means.

The Archetypal Dream: If you think that some of the material in your dreams is archetypal, one of the best places to look for its meaning is in the Bible. The reason for this is that the Bible contains some record of almost every archetypal experience that man can have.

Be Practical and Realistic: Do not necessarily look for the interpretation of dream material among the secret, hidden, very esoteric things. Usually, the opposite will apply; the meaning will be of a very common and familiar nature. Always try to reduce the symbology to the most simple terms. If you dream of a flashy car, for example, just ask yourself what flashy cars symbolize to you. If you dream of finding money, ask yourself what finding money is and means in waking life. If you dream of a church, ask yourself what the meaning of a church is to you in real life, etc. Be practical and realistic.

Lessons and Morals: Remember that your dreams are basically your inner reactions to the problems, conflicts, paradoxes and other situations that confront you in real life. They frequently will contain lessons and morals that are applicable to that life. For example, when dreaming of a past experience, it is likely that the dream is a warning that you may be presently in a situation similar to the past one and to beware of repeating the same or similar errors that you made then. So, whatever you dream, ask yourself, "Is there a moral or a lesson for me in this dream?"

The Illogical: Usually some material appears to be illogical. Even if only a fragment does not seem to fit, there are reasons for this. The dream could be reflecting something that actually is illogical in the dreamer's life. Or, some fear or mental block may be erasing the memory of a part of the dream. In any case, the same advice as that for unusual messages applies. Go to sleep the next time with the self-suggestion that you are seeking added meaning.

Look for Recurring Themes: The recurring dream usually means that the inner condition that is represented in the dream remains uncorrected or undealt with. Continued effort toward discovery of the causes of the dream is warranted. You may be refusing to face something, or ignoring the obvious. The dream may be giving you a way out of a dilemma that you do not really want to get out of. It may be telling you about a mistake that you do not want to admit. It may be telling you about a still unfulfilled childhood desire or about a complex that actually is quite difficult to deal with. Continue to seek the meaning. When you find it and do something about it, the dream is very likely to cease.

Look for Progress: Actively look for the progress you are making. Review your diary frequently. Compare the dreams of a month ago with the dreams of yesterday. In your daily entries or periodic summaries, make written notes of which fears seem lessened, which frustrations are not bothering you as much, etc. Progress, of course, is the whole aim of your interpretation program.

Look for ESP: Do not discount the possibility that some of your dream material may indeed be transpersonal or telepathic, or even prophetic—as well as personally predictive as already described. Most of your dreams will be of a personal and immediate nature. But there are too many cases of ESP in dreams on record for you to reject it out-of-hand.

Analyze Every Day: The best program of interpretation is the one in which you actively participate on a daily basis. So spend some time each day reading over your diary and attempting to see meaning in its contents. Frequently, new meaning will be added to older events—both from new dreams and from the added insights that you will be gaining as you progress in your own knowledge.

Awakening During the Night: With your notebook handy at your bedside, if you awaken during the night, reach for it and quickly jot down key words for the main characters, events and symbols in your dream. These will serve to trigger your memory for fuller recording in the morning. Never leave any dream unrecorded.

Prayer and Trust: There are very few people who take their own unconscious and its activities seriously who ultimately do not come to a realization of God Himself. The reason for this is fairly simply stated. The unconscious probably comes closer to what we commonly call the spiritual realm of our beings than most other aspects of life here on earth. You may not be a religious person. You may have your own definition of God. He doesn't mind; neither do we. The only thing of which we are absolutely certain is that "He" is here—and there. Simply because you do not see Him or have not experienced Him personally has no bearing whatsoever on the reality of his existence. We have yet to observe a single case where a person who earnestly sought Him did not find Him. Further, we have yet to observe a single case where a person who earnestly probed into his own being did not ultimately find Him.

It is thus our further recommendation that as you go to sleep, as a part of your meditative and autosuggestive practice, you also open yourself up to the possibility that you might meet God Himself in your own unconscious. Better yet, if you can at this point in your life, place yourself in His hands as you enter this world—trusting in the ultimate harmony that can come within it. God, like you, has many faces, many selves and forms, as recorded in the Bible, appears in "diverse places and ways." Do not be afraid to ask for guidance from outside of yourself.

Awaken With Thanks: Finally, commensurate with the whole feeling of openness and trust with which you must approach the understanding of your inner unconscious and the dreams that emerge from it, awaken each morning with thanksgiving in your heart for another night spent safely and alive—and for that which will be given you in the coming days and nights.

I want to convert my dreams into realities as far as possible.

Mahatma Gandhi

12

Dream Symbols
(A Dream Language Primer)

As explained throughout this book, dreams speak in a symbolic rather than a verbal language. The reason for this is that the unconscious has no need for words, since it already has stored within it the actual image or experience that it is trying to express or convey in the dream. There is another important difference between dream language and the everyday verbal language that we use in waking life. In our waking language, words, although they frequently have personalized connotations, basically have a one-for-one meaning. They convey essentially the same ideas to anyone who hears them. For example, everyone knows what you mean when you say "car," or "man," or "book," etc.

In dreams, however, this is not necessarily true. There need not be any "this-equals-that" translation of a symbol. A car may not be a car for the person who dreams about it, or a book, a book. One cannot even say that water, for example, always equals water, or always equals the unconscious, or certain fears; or that flying always means wanting to get above something; or that every elongated shape is a phallic symbol. What any symbol means always must be interpreted in terms of what it means to *the dreamer*, in *his* current psychic situation, in his overall life.

Certain symbols have consistently been found to mean the same or similar things to a great many dreamers. This, of course, is because many things do have a universal symbology which naturally would carry over into personal dreams. For example, it is easy to see that a book might have something to do with knowledge or learning, perhaps a need or desire for them; or that a car or other vehicle is transitional, having to do with going or changing from one position to another; or that water is something that is often deep and dark, smooth or rough on the surface or underneath, perhaps much like the human psyche or a part of it. Thus, a certain universality of symbology is inferable. It is also valid to seek to know what something in one's own dream has meant to other dreamers. In many cases, there will be a high probability that it may mean something similar.

Thus, although we have repeatedly cautioned against merely trying to look up the meaning of dream language on a one-for-one basis, additional insight can be found from this approach. At least you may find it a good starting point from which to determine your own meaning from a given symbol in your own dreams. For these reasons, we have compiled a list of common objects, occurrences and experiences into a dream language primer, with a combination of their universal meanings and what we have found many of them to mean in the dreams of people we have known. These are listed in the following pages.

HOW TO USE THE LIST

First: Before looking up any object, symbol, action, etc., in this listing, state in your dream diary entry what meaning this particular item has for you, irrespective of what it might mean either universally or to another dreamer. Always look first for the *personal* associations and relationships. Also, *go with your own feelings* of what something means to you *over* any other meaning. In all probability, this will be the most significant meaning.

Second: Move into a second level of thinking, without any external reference such as this listing. If you do not find any specific personal reference or association, try to *develop* a meaning of your own just by thinking about what you have seen in your dream. What do food, or wine, for example, mean to you irrespective of what they might mean in this dream? You may come up with a meaning such as the security of the home, companionship, conviviality, warmth, celebration, etc. Wine, too, may have some inherent religious symbology for you. In other words, seek the most natural symbology *within yourself* by reasoning it out based on your own thought and experience. What you are really saying is what this symbol means to *you*, in your own mind. Where will that meaning come from? It will come from the same source that your dream came from, within your psyche. Therefore, it is quite likely to have the same meaning that it had in your dream. At the very least, this will be a more valid meaning than someone else, including the authors, can give you. You will be much closer to your true personal interpretation.

Third: Look up the item in the following list and compare your meaning with the generalized meaning given. We have made this easy to do by providing space for you to write your meaning next to ours. Make an evaluation. For example, if the symbol for which you are seeking meaning is a house, you would combine the general idea of house as a possible representation of self (the house of self, if you will) with its representation of "home" and all of the associations that would go with this idea. You would also evaluate the particular house you dreamed of and what it means to *you personally*. Was it a mansion? Was it a fearsome place, a welcoming, hospitable place, etc.? If your dream contains symbols that are not listed here, try to think of a larger category to which that item belongs or something that is synonymous with it. A shed, for example, also fits into the larger category of house. If you were to dream of riding high above some mountains in a cable car (which is not listed), another step in your reasoning process could equate both car and flying. A movie and a play would be synonymous, a book and a magazine, etc. Generally speaking, whenever a person appears in a dream, it will be wise to consider the possibility that it is a shadow, persona, anima, animus or archetypal figure. After you have made this evaluation, the description of that type of person in the listing (a policeman, a judge, a doctor, etc.) can be used to gain further insight into your own meaning.

Also, when an event, emotion, circumstance, etc., is being considered, you must always analyze whether this represents a fear of or a desire for that particular happening. For example, dreaming of yourself as being a child, or dreaming of sailing in a boat, could be expressive of either an inner fear of doing or being these things—or, it could mean that you want, need or desire to do them within your inner self. Usually, the context of the rest of the dream—for instance, your feelings about what is happening, the violence or peacefulness of the occasion, etc.—will give you the clue as to the exact nature of the expression.

It is wise to share your dreams with some significant other person who can react to your personal observations and interpretations. Sometimes it will be necessary for you to approach one trained in analysis to help bring out some of the meanings that lie within the unconscious. But for the person who has trouble starting a chain of associations that seem pertinent to his situation, we hope this list will be suggestive.

COMMON DREAM SYMBOLS

Their Generalized Meanings and What They Have Meant in Some Dreams
and Your Personal Meaning

Our Meaning	Your Meaning
ABANDONMENT: To discard something, e.g., an old habit. A warning to do so. A fear of being lost or abandoned, of giving up something. To feel forsaken.	
ABYSS: Frequently may signify fear, danger, warning. Also may symbolize fear of falling. Fear of the unconscious. Depth. Death.	
ADULTERY: Sin. Often guilt-associated. Something forbidden. The literal sexual act.	
AIRPLANE: Movement. Travel. Progress. Advancing. Getting above things. Sometimes war or strife, depending on type. Altitude, conditions, etc., also significant.	
ALCHEMY: Changing the baser into the more precious. Transformation. Conjunction. Joining. Magical acts. Mystical thoughts and ideas.	
AMPUTATION: To cut off or sever. Symbolic of parts of personality. Often signifies depression, despair, fear of loss.	
ANCHOR: Something that stabilizes or holds. The implication is restrainment in time of stress. Also signifies salvation or rescuing.	

Our Meaning	Your Meaning
ANGEL; A messenger, an emmissary. Implies a profound message, tidings or news.	
ANGER: Dissatisfaction with part of self. Fear.	
ANIMALS: Generally represent the physical and sensory. Often sexual. See specific types.	
ANTS: Proverbially represent industry. Also may represent a complex of small bits of uncoordinated or ill-organized mental or emotional energy. Conversely may represent organization and regimentation. Multiplicity.	
ANUS: Childhood. Sometimes filth or excrement. Self-consciousness. Sometimes sexual. Often related to health or concern with bodily functions.	
APPLE: Earthly desires. Indulgence (from Adam and Eve myth). Also may represent freshness and newness. See also eating.	
ARGUMENT: Persons involved are significant. Internal conflict. Frustration or confusion in one's thinking. See also hitting.	

Our Meaning	Your Meaning
ARM: Work, strength, protection. Activity in general. The mode of use is significant, e.g., striking, vengeful acts, belligerence, protection, etc.	
ARROW: A weapon. Piercing. Hurting. Straightness. Also flies through the air. May represent directness.	
ARTIFACTS: Remnants. Perhaps ancient. Each has its own meaning or symbology. Generally, evidence of work or industry. May be religious in meaning.	
ASCENDING: May represent beginning (e.g., rising sun) or birth. Higher values. Virtue. Overinflated opinion of self. See also climbing; stairs; mountain; hill.	
ATTIC: Something upper and above. The mind. Oldness. Things stored away or forgotten.	
AUTHORITY: Depends upon type or figure, e.g., civil, religious, military, parental. Both fear of and desire to please. Respect or escape.	
AUTOMOBILE: Going somewhere. Power. Ego extension. Sometimes a feminine symbol. May represent personal acquisitiveness. Fear of losing. See also bus; train.	

Our Meaning	Your Meaning
AUTUMN: Change. End of period or season. Harvest. Preparation. Briskness. Feasting. Thanksgiving.	
AXE: A tool. Cutting. Cleaving. Splitting. Work. Industriousness. Also weapon. Perhaps a divine tool or weapon.	
BABY: Newness. Weakness. Immaturity. See also child.	
BANDAGES: Ministering. Healing. Medicating. Binding up wounds or splits. Also fear of being hurt.	
BASKET: Feminine symbol. A receptacle. Gather. Collecting. Receiving. Very ancient.	
BAT: Fear of night. Darkness. Sinister feeling. Ambiguity. Contraction.	
BATHING: Purification. Cleanness. Rejuvenation. Renewal. Change. Destruction. Need for renewing.	
BATTLE: Conflict. Inner strife. Confusion. Opposing parts of self.	
BEACH: Beginning and end. Embarkation. Transition. Edge of the unconscious. See also water; ocean.	
BEAUTY: Goodness. Spirituality. Personal adjustment. Good mind. Proper orientation. A cover-up or facade.	

Our Meaning	Your Meaning
BED: Womb. Cradle. Rest. Sex. Repose. Security. Night.	
BELLY: The middle or center. "Gut feelings." The place where transmutation takes place. Vulnerability. Antithetical to the brain. Visceral reaction.	
BIRDS: Thoughts. Children. Beneficence. Spirits. Flights of fantasy.	
BIRTH: Newness. New life. Beginnings. Regeneration.	
BITE: Feminine action or weapon. Primitive combat. Hostility. Tearing. Eating.	
BLACK: Absence of light. Death. Passivity. The unknown. The unconscious.	
BLOOD: Life. Power. Sacrifice. Fear of injury. Heredity, e.g., "blood will tell." Closeness of relationship.	
BLUE: Coolness. Serenity. Expansiveness. Openness. Thinking. Clarity of thought.	
BOAT: Transition. Relates to symbology of water. Seeking. The personal self. The womb or cradle.	
BODY: Life. Physical. Living. Death. Health. Seat of appetite. Materialism.	
BONE: Structure. Order. That which gives pattern or firmness. Indestructibility. Also symbolic of belief in resurrection.	

Our Meaning	Your Meaning
BOOK: Knowledge. Learning. Power. Spiritualism. The unknown.	
BOSS: Authority. Fear. Desire for authority.	
BOTTLE: Feminine symbol. That which things are put into. Sometimes clearness of vision. Also may be a phallic symbol.	
BOX: Female symbol. Keeping. Containing. Contents significant. The unconscious. See also container.	
BOY: Youth. Inferiority. Hope. Emerging masculinity. See also baby; child.	
BREAKING: Changing the form of something. Fragmenting. Conflict.	
BREATHING: Life. Spiritual power. Flux. Change. Dualism (in out). May symbolize difficulty in learning or knowing.	
BRIDGE: A connection, perhaps of thoughts or feelings. Putting separate things together. Reconciliation. Contract or covenant. Transition. Change or desire for change.	
BROOM: Need for order and cleansing.	
BROTHER: Commonality. Equality of relationship.	

Our Meaning	Your Meaning
BROWN: Earth. Excrement. Sometimes dirtiness. Mundaneness. Boredom. Fertility.	
BUILDING: Female symbol. Type and use significant. Self.	
BULL: Sensuality and power. Superiority. Zodiac symbol—Taurus. Universal symbol in all cultures.	
BURNING: Consuming. Destroying. Refining. May relate to sexual passion. Heat and light. See also fire.	
BURY: To cover or put away something. In a positive sense to hide for safe keeping. In the negative sense to try to eliminate or forget something. May imply that certain things have not been clear to one (e.g., they were buried).	
BUS: Means of transportation. Transitional. A group relationship may be indicated. Possibly a complex within one's self. See also train; automobile.	
CAGE: Confinement. Restriction. Inhibition. Failure to grow or mature. Get clue from what is in cage.	
CALENDAR: Cycling. Phases. Passing through a stage of life.	
CAMERA: Keeping a record. Proving or documenting. Desire to see more.	

Our Meaning	Your Meaning
CANDLE: Sometimes sexual or religious. Shedding light. Gaining knowledge. Fear of darkness or unknown. Individualism as opposed to generality of thought or feeling.	
CANNIBALISM: Self consumption, e.g., "eating yourself up with worry."	
CARPET: Cover-up. Hiding. Treading underfoot. Disdain.	
CASTLE: Protection. Ego defensiveness. Complexity. See also building.	
CASTRATION: Fear of loss of power. Particularly loss of sexual power.	
CAT: Sexuality. Duality. Sneakiness. Mysticism. Hidden meaning. Death. Warning.	
CAULDRON: Trouble. Inner seething or conflict. Purifying or preparing.	
CAVE: Feminine symbol. Concealed feeling. Security. The unconscious. Inner self. Secretness.	
CELLAR: The unconscious. Hidden emotion. Desire or conflict.	
CENTER: Interior. Unity. Gathering. Selfishness. Inner self.	

Our Meaning	Your Meaning
CHAIN: Connection. Restraint. Lack of freedom. Inhibition. Unity. Blood relationship. Bonds and obligations.	
CHAOS: Disorganized inner self. Lack of individuation. Undifferentiated emotions.	
CHILD: Desire for youth. Newness. Anticipation. Return to past. Simplicity. Youthful reawakening. The internal child self. See also baby.	
CHOKING: Fear of dying. Obstacles. Failure. Improper internal functioning. Groping.	
CHRIST: God. Divinity. Inner revelation. An announcement of a message.	
CHURCH: Desire or fear of God or own spirituality.	
CIRCLE: Wholeness. Continuation. Seeking. Maturity. God. Self. Unity.	
CITY: Progress. Culture. Interchange. Communication. Maturity. Hope for eternal life or permanence. Security.	
CLERGYMAN: Desire or fear of God or own spirituality. See also authority; minister; rabbi; priest.	
CLIMATE: General psychic situation.	

Our Meaning	Your Meaning
CLIMBING: Achieving. Struggling. Working. Desire.	
CLOCK: Anxiety. Lateness. Life, Motion. Transition. "Later than you think." Warning.	
CLOTHING: Covering. Protection. Hiding from something. Status. Rank.	
CLOUDS: Elevation. Fecundity. Growth. Expressiveness. Change.	
CLOWN: The archetypal trickster figure. The opposite of the serious and mature self. Often the victimized figure.	
COAT: Covering. Warmth, Outer personality. See clothing.	
COLDNESS: Isolation. Lack of emotion. Longing for solitude or exaltation. Lack of love. Dehumanization. Loneliness.	
COLORS: Signifies intensity. See individual colors.	
COLUMN: Male sexual symbol. Support. Soundness. Basis for sound reasoning.	
CONTAINER: Female symbol. See box; house; enclosure.	
CORNUCOPIA: Hope or desire for plenty. Prosperity. Fecundity. Fertility. Need for fulfillment.	

Our Meaning	Your Meaning
COUNTRYSIDE: Openness. Freedom. Relief. Reconciliation. Pleasure. Peace.	
COW: Tameness. Physical. Contentness. Docility. Slowness. Dullness. Opposite of sharp thinking. Abundance. Sexuality. Wish for peace.	
CRAWLING: Debasing self. Animal-like movement. Subservience. Immaturity or difficult terrain. Negotiating difficulties.	
CREEK: Living. Movement. Freshness. Flowing. Transition. Implication of larger water. See also water.	
CREMATION: A destructive part of personality. Excessive nervous energy. Desire to eliminate part of self.	
CRESCENT: Latent creativity. Growth or emergence. Change. Utopian wish.	
CRIME: Disruption. Discordant feelings. Inner conflict. Aggression. Illicit desire.	
CRISIS: Flood of obstacles. Failure in communications. Dangerous opportunity.	
CROSS: Transition. Lack of or desire for unity. Religion. Spirituality.	

Our Meaning	Your Meaning
CROSSROADS: Need for decision. Transition or conflict. Fear of deciding.	
CROW (raven): Beginnings. Maternal night. Fertility. Symbol of evil and mystery. See also birds.	
CROWD: Symbolic superiority. Totality and wholeness. Mood may denote mood of internal selves. Undifferentiated complexes, fears, etc. Multiplicity. Extraordinariness.	
CROWN: Elevation of self. Awe. Authority. Preeminence. Achievement. Egotism.	
CRYING: A warning. Sometimes foreboding. Anticipation of strife. Fear of loss. Expressing pent-up emotion. Can be recuperative or redemptive.	
CRYSTAL: Light. Spirituality. Transparency. Superficiality. Conjunction of opposites. Lack of resistance. Readiness for change.	
CUP: Female symbol. Nourishment. Counting of blessings. Emptiness or fullness is significant.	
CUTTING: Separation. Division. Lack of reconciliation. Individuation.	
DANCE: Celebration. Happiness. Worship. Sexuality. Union.	

Our Meaning	Your Meaning
DARKNESS: The unconscious. Fear. Death. The unknown. The inferior.	
DAUGHTER: Femaleness. Childhood. Desire for youth. Subservience or inferiority.	
DEAFNESS: Not being able to hear. Out of touch. The unknown. Warning to listen.	
DEATH: Finality. Fear of ego cessation. Desire to end something. Renewal. Going into unconscious.	
DECAPITATION: Fear of loss of reasoning power.	
DEFECATION: Excrement. Desire to repel part of self. Baseness.	
DENTIST: The head. Thinking. Symbolic loss of power through lost teeth. See also doctor.	
DEPTH: The unconscious. Need. Desire or reluctance to go into self. Desire or reluctance to have profoundness. Desire or reluctance to look into past.	
DESCENDING: Going into the unconscious. Baseness. Turning away higher ideals. Getting feet on ground.	
DESERT: Being lost. Loneliness. Despair. Lack of growth. Unfertile.	

Our Meaning	Your Meaning
DESK: Activity and work. Location, shape, and contents are significant.	
DESTRUCTION: Ambivalence. Conflict. Desire to eliminate part of self. Escape.	
DEVIL: Dark side of God. Evil. May be shadow figure or animus. Regression. Diversity. Disillusionment. Obstacles. Warning. Lying to self. Confusion. Chaos. Fragmentation. Inferiority. Perversion.	
DIAMOND: Desire for light or enlightenment. Desire for wealth. Probing a mystery.	
DIGESTION: Mastery. Assimilation. Dissolution. Rejection. Acceptance. Vomiting.	
DIRT: Dirty. Earth. Revulsion. The base and lowly parts.	
DISGUISE: Persona. Hiding from truth or reality. May indicate sexual perversion.	
DISHES: Eating. Celebration. Feast. Conviviality. Family closeness.	
DISK: Heaven. Perfection. See also circle.	
DISMEMBERMENT: Disintegration of self. Breakdown. Ill health. Need to eliminate destructive tendency in personality.	

Our Meaning	Your Meaning
DOCTOR: Healing. Health problem. Desire for wholeness. See also dentist.	
DOG: Sensuality. Faithfulness. Symbol of valor. Guardianship.	
DOLL: Ineffective or inactive human figure. Superficiality. May indicate a complex of energy.	
DOORWAY: Entering or exiting into a phase. Fear of entering or exiting. See also threshold.	
DOVE: Spirituality. Peace. Sublimation. See also birds.	
DRAGON: A universal symbol. Amalgam of aggressive feelings. The monster in self.	
DRESS: See clothing.	
DRINKING: Refreshment. Desire for newness or renewal. Substance being ingested is significant.	
DROPPING: A self-warning. Losing some part of self. Not meeting responsibilities.	
DROWNING: Going into subconscious. Fear of unconscious self. Desire to eliminate part of self. Loss of life force. Return to womb.	

Our Meaning	Your Meaning
DRYNESS: Lack. Desolateness. Thirst. Desire. See also desert.	
DUMMY: Dehumanization. Primitive image of soul—especially in voodoo magic. Inactivity or nonparticipation. May be a persona.	
EAGLE: Height. Spirituality. The symbol par excellence for all birds. Mystical power and authority. Victory. See also birds.	
EARTH: A basic female principal. Fertility. Growth. Fecundity. Light. Primitiveness. Also occasionally motherhood.	
EARTHQUAKE: A cataclysm. A warning of impending, crisis. A sudden change in a given process or the personality. Pent-up power and emotion. See also explosion.	
EATING: Taking nourishment. Pleasant sensation. Warning regarding diet. Sensuality. Materialism.	
EGG: A basic female symbol. Fertility. Newness. Birth. Potential. Mystery. Sometimes indicates a thought or feeling trying to make itself known. See also circle; fruit.	
EIGHT: The symbol of newness, resurrection or change.	

Our Meaning	Your Meaning
ELEPHANT: Power. Wisdom. Desire for long life.	
ELEVATOR: Arising. Box or enclosure. Restricted rising. See also climbing.	
ELEVEN: Transition. Excess. Peril. Conflict.	
EMBRACING: Hugging. Kissing. Fondling. Need for acceptance. Approval or affirmation. Also may symbolize a desire for knowing. Insight. Growth.	
EMOTION: Each emotion felt in a dream is symbolic of itself, e.g., fear, hate, hostility, friendliness, etc.	
EMPTINESS: Superficiality. Fear of being lost. Lack of fulfillment.	
ENCLOSURE: Type is the key. See building; house; cage; elevator; jail; castle.	
ENGINE: Power. Desire for power or strength. May be symbolic of the body or internal organs. See force.	
ENJOYMENT: Usually symbolizes well-being or adjustment within the context of the dream. Festivity. Ecstacy.	

Our Meaning	Your Meaning
ENTANGLEMENT: Complexes. Inner confusion. Trapped feeling. Ensnared. Caught in someone else's scheme.	
ESCAPING: Fear. Running away from a problem or a threat. Retreat from a decision or course of action.	
EVENING: The end of day. Peace. Stillness. Tranquility. Desire for rest or escape.	
EXCREMENT: Desire to eliminate an undesirable aspect of self. Self-dislike. Transmutation. See also defecation; urination.	
EXPLOSION: Fear. Impending disintegration. Cataclysm. Release of pent-up emotions.	
EYE: To observe. To understand. To be exposed. To seek insight. To be watched. Ancient symbol for God.	
FACES: A confrontation. Outward show of inner feeling. Or emotion. Also may be a mask or persona.	
FACTORY: Activity. Industriousness. Making and creating, perhaps new parts of self. See also work.	
FAIRY: Desire for miraculous help. Magic. An appeal to some supernatural force. A personal desire for extraordinary power.	

Our Meaning	Your Meaning
FALLING: Diversion from true purpose. Fear of failure. Warning of a wrong decision or course in life.	
FARMER: The simpler part of one's personality. Connection with the earth. Desire for return to simplicity. Rejection of complexity. Fertility. Growth. Desire for regeneration.	
FATHER: A basic masculine principal. Corresponds to consciousness as opposed to unconsciousness. A need for leadership or a reluctance to mature. Tradition, sound thinking, morality, etc.	
FEAR: Can mean many things depending on what is feared.	
FEAST: Orgiastic experience or overindulgence. A warning of overindulgence. Celebration. See also eating; food.	
FEATHER: Wind. Spirituality. Lightness of spirit. Sometimes associated with a desire to fly or rise above things.	
FENCE: A boundary. A border. An inhibition. Depends on what or who is inside or outside of fence. See also enclosure.	
FIELD: Openness. Freedom. A sense of release. A sense of limitless potentiality. Generally a positive image.	

Our Meaning	Your Meaning
FIGHT: Inner conflict between parts of self. Ego-defensiveness. Opposites or elements within the personality.	
FINGERS: Sorting things. Counting. Small parts of personality. Sometimes animal characteristics, such as scratching, clawing, grasping. Holding onto something like a fear or complex.	
FIRE: Cleansing. Death. Resurrection. Destruction. Life. Desire for superiority or control. Power. See also burning.	
FISH: One of oldest Christian symbols. Signifies nourishment. Penetrative motion. Getting into the unconscious. A desire to return to the simpler, purer motives of life.	
FIVE: Symbolic of man, health and love. The five senses. The two arms, two legs plus the head and reasoning powers.	
FLAG: Expresses exaltation and inflation, or the desire to heighten feeling or emotion. A totem. The flagpole also is important and the position of the flag.	
FLOOD: Destruction. Fear of being engulfed by emotions or other forces. Fear of seeing into one's own unconscious.	

Our Meaning	Your Meaning
FLOOR: Substance. Foundation. Firmness.	
FLOWER: Desire for beauty. To blossom. To grow. Newness. Fertility. Fulfillment.	
FLYING: A very complex symbol. Wishful thinking. Desire to rise above a problem or a lower part of self. Sometimes symbolizes sex. Transcendency. Growth. Fantasy. Space. Thought. Imagination.	
FOG: Confusion. Perplexity. Partiality of awareness. Thoughts or feelings attempting to emerge. Sometimes the edge of the unconscious. That which is hidden.	
FOOD: See eating.	
FOOL: A very old symbol. Sometimes a sinner. The foolish part of one's personality. Incoherence. Confusion. Rejection of sound thinking. The irrational part of the personality. Blind impulse.	
FOOT: Ambivalence. Relationship with the earth. Sometimes phallic or sexual. Transition. Going somewhere. Support. Soundness of opinion, e.g., "feet on the ground."	
FORCE: Meaning will be implied in the dream itself depending on kind of force.	

Our Meaning	Your Meaning
FOREST: The unconscious position of dreamer is significant, e.g., on the edge or within. May represent primitive self.	
FOUNTAIN: The source of wisdom. Life. Renewal. Comfort. Origins and beginnings. See also water.	
FOUR: Related to the circle. Transition. Unity. Harmony. Balance. Feminine characteristics.	
FROG: Connection with the natural. Connection with water and its representations of the unconscious. Sometimes a leaping and hopping aspect of one's personality. Transition from water to earth and breathes air. Change and adaptation.	
FRUIT: Equivalent to egg. Represents origin. Earthly appetites. Some relationship to health.	
FUEL: Power. Warmth. Desire for energy. Relates sometimes to sun and cosmic forces.	
FURNITURE: Type and location are keys to interpretation. Basically pertains to something inside of self. Possibly intellect, ability, gifts, shortcomings, etc.	
GAMES: A lack of seriousness in life. An unconscious desire to avoid facing real problems. Need for play or recreation.	

Our Meaning	Your Meaning
GARDEN: Nature. Growth. Fertility. Subdued or controlled natural forces, perhaps within self. Also may be symbol of consciousness.	
GIANT: Often ego inflation. An overdeveloped part of self. Probably a shadow figure. Sometimes fear of or need for authority.	
GIRL: Basically unspoiled femaleness. See also child; daughter.	
GLOBE: Basically a symbol for wholeness. A desire for wholeness and unity or to "get to the center of things." Also may be an archetypal symbol. See also circle; egg; fruit; etc.	
GLOVES: Often signify a desire to cover up bad things done with the hands in conscious life. Hiding something, usually from self. Also may signify self-protection or self-defense.	
GLUE: To stick together or to seek cohesiveness. May be associated with sperm or sexual intercourse.	
GOD: In a dream usually a desire for higher spirituality or a fear of discovery. See authority.	
GOLD: Something precious. Materialism. Higher thoughts or sublime or noble feelings. Image of light. Intelligence and knowledge.	

Our Meaning	Your Meaning
GOVERNMENT; May be that regimented unreasoning part of self. May signify conscious control of self as opposed to baser instinct and desires. See also authority.	
GRAPES: Fertility. Gathering or grouping of characteristics associated. Growth. See also fruit; globe; circle; egg.	
GRAVE: The unconscious. Death. Desire or fear of ego cessation.	
GREEN: Life. Newness. Immediacy. Growth. Sensation.	
GUARD: The protective part of the personality. Reluctance to see some deeper meaning or feeling within self.	
GUN: Often a phallic symbol. Symbolizes power or strength. The desire to kill some part of one's self. To destroy an undesirable situation in life.	
HAIR: The head. Reasoning. Covering. Loss of may symbolize fear of age or loss of strength or virility.	
HALO: Religious awe. Wholeness. Determinism. Desire for guidance.	
HAMMER: Power. Strength. Hostility. Aggression.	
HANDS: Work. The personality. Frenzy. Health problem. "Dirty work."	

Our Meaning	Your Meaning
HANDSHAKING: Confrontation. Embracing shadow self.	
HANGING: Death wish for part of self. Self-denial. Sacrifice.	
HARDNESS: An obstacle. Confrontation. A desire to penetrate. See also sensory experience.	
HAT: The head. Higher reasoning. Grouping of ideas. Getting ideas into the head. Hidding ideas. See also clothing.	
HATE: Literal. Also dislike of part of self. Cover for fear.	
HAWK: The soul. Thoughts. Aggressiveness. Sexuality. See also birds.	
HEADLESS: Nonreasoning. Hidden. Unidentified fears or parts of self.	
HEART: The center. Health. Spirituality. Power.	
HEAT: Type and intensity is significant, e.g., the "fires of hell" as opposed to the warmth of a hearth and its associations.	
HEAVEN: Utopian wish. Spirituality. Intellectual light. Transition. Death wish.	
HEAVINESS: Emotional burden. Despair. Problems. Struggle. Great worth.	
HEIGHT: Inflation. Goals. See also flying; ascending.	

Our Meaning	Your Meaning
HEMISPHERE: Partiality Incompleteness. Duality. Sexuality. Birth and death. Balance.	
HERMAPHRODITE: Inner sexual conflict. Duality. Complexes. Opposites. Desire for wholeness.	
HERO: Exalted part of self. Desire to achieve or reach perfection. See also authority.	
HILL: Fear of or desire for elevation. Goals. Overinflation. Rising above things. See also ascending; climbing.	
HITTING: Hostility. Aggression. Desire to hurt or attack part of self.	
HOLE: The unconscious. Universal female symbol. Wholeness. Fear of or desire for past. Newness. Opening. Transition.	
HOOD: Hiding. Hidden parts. Embarrassment. Repression.	
HOPE: Unfulfilled wish. Self-delusion. Cover for lack of action.	
HORSE: Sensuality. Power. Transition. Baseness. Swiftness. Hurrying.	
HORNS: Evil. Sensuality or animalism. The devil. Prosperity. "Above the head." Reasoning power.	

Our Meaning	Your Meaning
HOSPITAL: Health. Death wish. Fear of illness. Desire for security.	
HOUSE: The self. Type is significant. Universal female symbol. Security. Hidden rooms or parts of self.	
HUGGING: Confrontation. Embracing parts of self. Need for affection.	
HUNGER: Literal, or for spiritual or mental nourishment. Emptiness. Loneliness.	
HUNTER: Duality. The chase. Sexuality. Escape. Egress from the center or from open confrontation.	
HURRICANE: Inner turmoil. Conflict. Complexes.	
HUSBAND: Maleness. Authority. Security. Strength. Personal relationship is key. See also father.	
ICE: Coldness. Relief and rest. Thirst. Loneliness. Isolation. See also sensory experience.	
INCEST: Union or unity. Conflict of parts of self. Desire for wholeness.	
INSECTS: Depends on type, e.g., stinging, benign, etc. Trivia. Being beset by many bothersome things. See also animals.	

Our Meaning	Your Meaning
INTERCOURSE: Sexuality. Desire for union or unity. Confrontation. Illness. A "sick" part of the personality.	
INTERSECTION: A decision. A merging of ideas. A conflict. Conjunction. Communication.	
INVISIBILITY: A desire to hide. Something that is hidden. Escape. Dissolution. The unconscious.	
ISLAND: An isolated part of the personality. Loneliness. A desire to see more clearly.	
JAIL: Restriction. Confinement. Desire to escape something. A trapped feeling. See also building; enclosure.	
JEWELRY: Sublimated thoughts. Light. Superficiality. Materialism. Wealth. Security.	
JOB: Industriousness. Fears, desire and hopes associated with same. See also work.	
JOURNEY: Transition. Desire to escape. Desire for a goal.	
JUDGE: Confrontation. Communication. Death. Illumination. Regeneration. Healing and resurrection. See also authority; father; king; minister; teacher.	

Our Meaning	Your Meaning
JUDGMENT: Confrontation. Guilt. Communication with parts of self. Authority. Fear of discovery.	
KEY: Unlocking mysteries. Finding hidden ideas or parts of self. Entering into new phases. May be phallic symbol. See also lock.	
KING: The stronger part of self. Elevation or overinflation. See also authority; father; judge; minister; teacher.	
KISSING: Intimate contact. Communication. Conjunction and unity of parts. See also embracing; hugging.	
KITCHEN: Home. Security. Warmth. Sustenance. See also eating.	
KNIFE: Cleavage or separation, e.g., of parts of the personality. Isolation. Death. A wish to cut off part of the personality. See also cutting.	
LABYRINTH: Confusion. Searching. Seeking a goal.	
LAKE: The unconscious. State of water and position of dreamer are significant, e.g., at the edge, atop or in the water.	
LAMB: Docility. Sexuality. Need for protection.	

Our Meaning	Your Meaning
LAMP: Individuated or concentrated enlightenment as opposed to generalized. See also light.	
LATENESS: A warning.	
LAUGHING: Literal. Happiness. Derision. Playing a trick on self.	
LEGS: Transition. Traveling. Movement. Duality. Sex. Sexuality. Firmness. See also amputation.	
LETTER: A message. A warning. Impending Disaster. A desire to learn.	
LIGHT: Literal. Clarity. Well-being. Confrontation. Communication. A seeking of experience or insight. See also yellow.	
LIGHTNESS: Relief. Self-adjustment. Well-being. Possible loss of contact with earth. Dizzyness. See also heaviness.	
LIGHTNING: A warning. A cataclysm. An explosive state. Enlightenment. Force.	
LION: Sensuality. Sexuality. Strength.	
LIQUOR: Intoxication. A drunken part of self. Desire for escape. Fantasy.	

Our Meaning	Your Meaning
LOCK: Something guarded. Protected. Hard to get at. Perhaps a hidden part of the personality or a fear. A feminine symbol. See also key.	
LONELINESS: Literal. A rejected part of self.	
LOSS (of an object): A part of self that is lost. Seeking something of value. Seeking enlightenment.	
LOST (being lost): Literal. Part of self being lost. Isolation. Separation.	
LUGGAGE: A general feminine symbol. Traveling. Transition. Need or desire for movement from one phase of life to another.	
MACHINES: Materialism. Dehumanization. Efficiency. Rhythm. The body.	
MANAGER: A need for or fear of authority. See also authority.	
MANDALA: A very complex symbol for wholeness, unity, or divinity. Religious experience. Confusion. Chaos. See also circle.	
MARRIAGE: Literal. Conjunction. Communication. Getting in touch with the unconscious or with other sides of the personality.	
MASK: Persona. Hiding a part of self. Seeking hidden meaning. A desire for transformation or metamorphosis. Secrecy.	

Our Meaning	Your Meaning
MAZE: Transition. Confusion. Loss. Seeking. Searching. Passageways. Hallways.	
MEADOW: Openness. Cl.ity. Earthiness. Release. Freedom.	
MEAT: Flesh. Fleshiness. Carnality. Life. Blood. Killing. Sexuality. See also eating.	
METALS: Each has its own symbolism, e.g., iron/hardness, gold/preciousness, mercury/illusiveness, tin/cheapness or superficiality, etc.	
METAMORPHOSIS: Transformation. Change for the better or the worse. Warning to change. Duplicity or multiplicity of personality.	
MICE: Smallness. A feeling of insignificance. Small parts of self. Fear of being trapped. Little irritations. See also rats.	
MILK: Sensuality. Nourishment. Security. Motherhood. Cleanliness.	
MINISTER: Usually with the religious association. See authority; father; manager; rabbi; teacher; priest.	
MIRROR: Confrontation. Seeing into self. The soul. The unconscious.	

Our Meaning	Your Meaning
MIST: Transition from one phase of thinking, feeling, or life to another. Becoming hidden. Being revealed.	
MOANING: A warning of inner trouble. Distress. Related to pain.	
MONEY: Materialism. Desire for goals. Superficiality. Seeking, finding, or losing something of value.	
MONKEY: Sometimes a darker side of the personality. Unconscious activity. The baser forces within one's self. Also certain magical qualities in some cultures.	
MONSTER: The unconscious. Wickedness. Conscience. Chaos. Confusion. The ultimate in animal sensuality.	
MOON: A universal symbol. Feminity. Unity. Wholeness. Mystery. Searching for the higher or more divine. Phase of the moon would indicate partiality of the various symbolic indications.	
MOTHER: A universal symbol. Desire for return to childhood. Security. Warmth. Any association with one's own mother. The earth. Productivity.	

Our Meaning	Your Meaning
MOTOR: See machines; engine; force.	
MOUNTAIN: Achievement. Rising above. Elevation or overinflation. Goals. Power. See also ascending; climbing; hill; descending.	
MOUTH: Sensuality. Animalism. The form of speech involved. Thinking. Rationalizing as opposed to feeling.	
MOVIE: An attitude toward life as superficial. Playacting. Escaping from problems and conflicts.	
MURDER: To kill part of self. To eliminate. See also grave; death.	
MUSIC: Type is significant. A very complex symbol. Personal associations are significant, e.g., the sound of a favorite song.	
MUSICIAN: Fascination with death or the unknown. Undifferentiated emotion.	
MUTENESS: Inability to communicate, confront, or embrace. Inability to define an inner problem.	

Our Meaning	Your Meaning
NAKEDNESS: Purity. Innocence. Exposure. Lewdness. Sexuality. Most nudity signifies an ambivalent and ambiguous emotion. Often indicates fear of exposure.	
NAMES: May indicate persona, masks, or superficiality. Identity.	
NIGHT: The unconscious. Darkness. The unknown.	
NINE: A triple synthesis. Three three's.	
NOTHINGNESS: The unconscious. Something lost or undiscovered. A yearning for substance. Loneliness.	
NUMBERS: The symbology of numerology is very complex and a whole volume would be necessary to explain it. See numbers one through twelve (and zero) in alphabetic listing for brief equation of symbology.	
NURSE: Health. Fear of illness. A sick part of self.	
NUT: Similar in symbology to various shapes. See egg; fruit; circle; planets.	

Our Meaning	Your Meaning
OCEAN: The unconscious. The condition of the sea or ocean is significant. See also lake.	
ODOR: May be externally induced while sleeping. Type of odor is the key, e.g., incense, repulsive smells, etc.	
OFFICE: May indicate petitioning, seeking help or advice, etc. See also work; job; and problems and conditions associated with same.	
OFFICERS: Desire for or fear of authority. See authority; father; manager; government; minister; teacher.	
OLDNESS: Old person, may be archetypal figure. Also fear of or respect for oldness or age. Desire for return to former times.	
ONE: Unity. Unbrokenness. Integration.	
OPENINGS: Basically a female symbol. Transition. Change. See also hole; doorway; threshold.	
ORGY: Literal, or orgy of parts of personality. Conflict. Confusion. Chaos. Sensuality.	

Our Meaning	Your Meaning
PAPER: A message. A warning. Superficiality or flimsiness.	
PARADE: Inner order. Loss of individuality.	
PARADISE: Desire for unity, rectitude, peace, or the existence of same within the individual.	
PAST: The unconscious. Childhood. Hidden complexes or desires.	
PENIS: Sensuality. Sexuality. Maleness.	
PHOTO: Probably a shadow figure.	
PIG: Literal symbology applies.	
PLANETS: A desire to attain or achieve. To move or change. See also circle.	
PLANT LIFE: Symbol of life. Birth. Nascent characteristics. Emerging parts of the personality. Renewal. Death. Resurrection. Fertility.	
PLAY (participating in): Frivolity. Desire to escape responsibility. Superficiality. Persona.	

Our Meaning	Your Meaning
POLICEMAN: See authority; father; manager; teacher; minister; government.	
POND: See ocean; lake.	
PREGNANCY: Desire to return to the womb. Fullness. Life. Turning inward on self.	
PRESIDENT: See authority; father; manager; government; teacher.	
PRIEST: An intercessor. Communication. Purgatory. Transition or change. See also authority; father; minister.	
PRISON: See jail.	
PROSTITUTE: Waking symbology applies. Prostituting one's self or higher being.	
PURPLE: Passions. Resurrection. Newness. Royalty or sovereignty. God or the divine. High church liturgy. Synthesis. Power. Spirituality and sublimation.	
PYRAMID: The basic symbology of the triangle or three. Also may be associated with mountain or hill depending on size.	

Our Meaning	Your Meaning
QUEEN: Femaleness. See also mother.	
QUEST: Any searching or seeking. Goals, attainment, peace, rectitude, etc.	
RABBI: Learning. Knowledge. Wisdom. See also authority; father; minister.	
RADIANCE: Awareness of numinous. See also light.	
RAIN: Cleansing. Growth. Being beset by many small or minor ills and troubles. Disintegration.	
RATS: Contamination. Baseness. Revulsion. See also mice.	
RED: Blood. Life. Fire. Heat. Surging or teeming emotions. Pulsation.	
RETURNING (from trip): Communication. Confrontation. Reconciliation. Desire to return to past.	
RIDING (horse): Sensuality. Transition. Masculinity.	

Our Meaning	Your Meaning
RING: See circle; jewelry; egg; fruit; planets.	
RISING: See ascending; climbing; mountain; hill; stairs; descending.	
RIVERS: The unconscious. Flowing. Growth. Transition and inner movement. See also ocean; lake; water.	
ROADS: Transition. Desire for change. Movement. Growth.	
ROBE: May indicate formality or stiffness. See also clothing.	
ROCK: Solidness. Substantiality. Solidarity. Cohesion.	
ROPE: Similar to the chain. A binding or connection or linking. Joining together. Saving. Salvation. Restriction or confinement.	
RUNNING (to or away): Frenzy. Fear. Anxiety. Desire to escape. Anxious to return or reunite.	
SACRIFICE (a ritual): Very primitive, perhaps archetypal. Death wish. Desire to eliminate something.	

Our Meaning	Your Meaning
SAILING: Freedom. Self. The unconscious. Fantasy. Transition.	
SAND: Coldness. Warmth. Loneliness. Playfulness. Diffusion. Openness.	
SCHOOL: Learning. Openness. Desire for enlightenment. Return to youth. See also building.	
SCISSORS: Decision. Death. Sexuality. Duality. Duplicity. Sharpness. Separation.	
SEARCH: Seeking. Desire for clarity. Fulfillment. Object is key.	
SENSORY EXPERIENCE: Content is key. May be caused by external stimuli while sleeping. Sensuality. Baseness.	
SEVEN: The ancient symbol of perfection.	
SEXUAL ORGANS: Literal. Fear of castration. Immasculinity. Femaleness. Desire for or fear of loss of sexuality.	
SHADOW: A part of self. Fear of unknown. See also darkness.	
SHARPNESS: Cutting. Separateness. Isolation. Clarity. Confrontation. Splitting away.	

Our Meaning	Your Meaning
SHIP: Self. Surface of the unconscious.	
SHOES: Transition. Need or want. "Feet on the ground." Escape. See also foot.	
SHOOTING: Killing. Deciding. Confronting. Sexual intercourse. See also murder.	
SHOUTING (or screaming): Fear. Invocation of help. Need for help. Warning.	
SINGING: Type is significant. Melancholy. Joy. Sorrow.	
SIREN (police car siren): Fear. Health. Death wish. Authority. Warning. Cataclysm.	
SISTER: Femaleness. Youth. Naiveness. Desire for youth.	
SITTING: Repose. Lack of fear. Apathy. Resignation. Giving up. Confidence.	
SIX: Ambivalence. Equilibrium. Compromise. Short of seven, lacks perfection.	
SKIPPING: Skipping something of significance or importance.	

Our Meaning	Your Meaning
SKULL: Death fear or wish. Pain. Sickness. Warning. Poisoning self. The mind. The head.	
SKY: Freedom. Enlightenment. Relief. Keys are condition of sky and position of dreamer.	
SLEEPING (dream of): Escape. Serenity. Sickness.	
SLIPPING: Impending danger. A self-warning.	
SLOGANS: Actual words are key. The rationale. Religion. Learning. Warning.	
SMOKE: Cover-up. Hiding. Transition from or to obscurity.	
SMOKING: Inner anxiety. Worry or despair.	
SNAKE: Evil. Sensuality. Baseness. Deceipt. Temptation.	
SNOW: Undifferentiated, diffused desire or fear. Covering up something.	
SOFTNESS: Key: what or who is soft. Resilience. Rest. Repose. Confidence. Indecision.	
SON: Youth. Desire. Simplicity. Dependence. Rebellion.	

Our Meaning	Your Meaning
SPACE: Loneliness. Desire for acceptance. Enlightenment. Fear of entrapment.	
SPINNING (rotating): Inner activity and turmoil. Power. Need to settle down. Escape.	
SPRINGTIME: Newness. Desire. Sensuality. Fertility.	
SQUARE: Unity. Earthiness. Spirituality. Balance.	
STAIRS: Direction and goal are key. See also climbing; ascending; descending.	
STANDING: Impatient. Strength. Security. Waiting.	
STAR: Light. Spirituality. Enlightenment. Individuation.	
STICK: Weapon. Fear. Phallus. Need for help.	
STORM: Inner turmoil. Fear. A complex or neurosis.	
STRANGER: Unknown part of self. Fear or desire to know. Need for self-confrontation.	
STREETS: Transition. Growth. Seeking.	

Our Meaning	Your Meaning
STRENGTH: Literal strength of feeling, or physical strength. What has the strength is key, e.g., self, authority, figure, shadow, etc.	
STRIKING: See hitting.	
SUCKING: Childishness. Sexuality. Desire for security. Immaturity.	
SUMMER: Enlightenment. Melancholy. Fantasy. Playfulness.	
SUN: God. Spirituality. Revelation. Openness. Knowledge. Enlightenment. See also light.	
SUPERIORITY (self): Cover for inferiority or inadequacy.	
SWIMMING: A healthy relation with the unconscious. Willingness to see, learn, change, confront self.	
SWORD: Phallic symbol. Power. Cutting. Cleavage. Inner conflict. Decision.	
TABLE: Eating. Nourishment. Gregariousness. Confrontation.	
TATOOING: Content is part of key. Need for power or recognition.	

Our Meaning	Your Meaning
TEACHER: Desire to learn. Maturity. Motherliness or fatherliness. See also authority; minister; rabbi; father.	
TEETH: Power. Strength. Virility or fear of losing. See also dentist.	
TELEKINESIS: Desire for power.	
TELEPHONE: A warning. A message. A need to communicate.	
TELEPORTATION: Desire for change. Enlightenment. Transition.	
TEN: Totality—metaphysical and material.	
THEATRE: Mental activity. Persona. Need for popularity. Laxness of moral standards. Sense of inner hypocrisy.	
THIEF: Robbing self. Desire to hide or eliminate something.	
THIRST: Literal. Desire for fulfillment or for spirituality. Despair. Need for inner cleansing.	
THREE: Spiritual synthesis. Sufficiency. Harmony. The number of God.	

Our Meaning	Your Meaning
THRESHOLD: Transition. Need for decision or confrontation. Newness. See also doorway.	
THRONE: Fear of condemnation. Desire for approval. See also authority.	
THUNDER: Power. Fear. Cataclysm. Confusion in thinking. See also explosion.	
TIGER: Sensuality. Aggressiveness. See also cat.	
TOES: Multiplicity of foundation. Health. See also foot; shoes.	
TOILET: Probably bowel trouble. May have sexual connotations.	
TOMB: The unconscious. See also grave.	
TOWER: Desire for achievement. Overinflation of self. Egotism. See also ascending.	
TOYS: Desire for escape. Hypocrisy. Superficiality. Lack of responsibility. Persona. Temptations.	
TRAIN: Transition. Lack of differentiation of personality. Dependence.	

Our Meaning	Your Meaning
TRANSFORMATION: Literal. Desire for or fear of change.	
TREASURE: The unconscious. Materialism. Desire. Something precious.	
TREE: Life. Growth. Living. Attracted to the earth.	
TRIANGLE: Sometimes unity and wholeness. The body. See also three; God; earth.	
TRIP: See journey.	
TURTLE: Slowness. Reluctance to change. Illness. Fertility. Sexuality. Longevity.	
TWELVE: Cosmic order and salvation. The notion of space and time and the wheel or circle.	
TWILIGHT: The twilight of enlightenment. An ending. A forthcoming or need for change. Rest. Peace. Rectitude. Reconciliation or resignation. See also mist; smoke; light.	
TWINS: Duplicity in self. Sexual intercourse.	
TWO: Echo. Reflection. Conflict. Counterbalance. Duality. Male/female.	

Our Meaning	Your Meaning
TYING (knots): Restraining part of self. Reluctance. See also chain; rope.	
UMBRELLA: Covering. Protection. Hiding.	
URINATION: Desire to expel. Sexual intercourse. Preoccupation with sex. Eliminating bad qualities. See also excrement.	
URN: Female sexuality. Domesticity. Docility.	
UTOPIA: Inner peace or desire for it. Self-adjustment. Childish fantasy.	
VALLEY: Going into unconscious. Inferiority. Protection. Contrast with mountain. The "valley of the shadow of death."	
VEGETABLE: Growth. Life. Sexuality. Physical appetite. Birth. Newness. See also plant life.	
VICTORY: Winning. Overcoming. Key is who wins. Confrontation. Individuation.	
VOMIT: Desire to expel the impure or unacceptable. See also urination; defecation; digestion.	

Our Meaning	Your Meaning
WALKING: Peaceful transition. Lack of fear.	
WAND (magic): The fantasized, unreal solution to a problem.	
WANDERING: Being lost. Seeking. Despair. Insecurity.	
WAR: Inner conflict. Desire to destroy. Undifferentiated anxiety.	
WASHING: Desire for cleansing. Change or reconciliation.	
WATER: Generally the unconscious. Position of dreamer is key. See also rivers; lake; ocean.	
WEATHER: Type signifies inner personal state.	
WEDDING: Duality. Sexual intercourse. Coming to terms with self. Decision. Transition.	
WEEPING: Despair. Fear. Compassion. Crying for part of self.	
WEIGHT: A burden. A problem. Worry or fear. Great worth. See also heaviness; lightness.	
WHEEL: The circle. Wholeness. Transition. Change.	

Our Meaning	Your Meaning
WHISTLE: A warning.	
WHITENESS: Clarity. Peace. Health or illness. Emptiness. Sterility.	
WIFE: To husband is herself, or desire for mother. Femaleness. Security. Sexual intercourse.	
WILDERNESS: Hopelessness. Meditativeness. Quest for spirituality. Isolation.	
WIND: Type is key. Openness. Lack of fear. Transition. Power.	
WINDOW: An opening or opportunity to change. Desire for change or transition. Contrast with door, e.g., looking into versus going into.	
WINE: Conviviality. Desire for warmth. Friendship. Acceptance. Celebration.	
WINGS: See flying.	
WINTER: Coldness. Lack of acceptance. Rejection. Desire to draw into self.	
WITCH: Femaleness. Bitchiness. Fear. Fantasized solution to problem. Lack of realism. Evil.	

Our Meaning	Your Meaning
WOLF: Hostility. Aggression. Sexuality. Carnal appetite. Anima or animus.	
WORK: Action. Self-improvement.	
X-RAY: Seeing into self.	
YELLOW: Light. Sun. Revelation. Intuition. Flashes of insight or illumination.	
YOUTH: Newness. Immaturity. Desire or need for renewal or regeneration.	
ZERO: Nonbeing. A symbol for wholeness and eternity.	

Index